Spiritual Restoration

Reclaiming The Foundations of God's World

Volume 2

By Skip Moen, D. Phil.

Copyright 2011

Be diligent to present yourself approved to God as a workman who does not need to be ashamed, accurately handling the word of truth. 2 Timothy 2:15 Sha'ul

More Torah, more life;
More study, more wisdom;
More counsel, more understanding;
More charity, more peace. Pirke Avot 2:8A Hillel

Dedicated to Rachel,
Serving in the United States Navy
On board the John C. Stennis

Reclaiming God's World

This is the second volume of a collection of my daily explorations of the vocabulary, culture and idioms found in biblical texts. Writing more than 3000 of these one-page editions has helped me recognize two crucial facts: first, most of us are so far removed from the history, culture and language of authors of the Bible that we don't understand what they were saying to their own audiences and secondly, most of us hunger to know God in a much deeper way. This second observation propels us to look beyond our simple English translations and ask what these words mean and why they were written. We long for the experience of His presence that we only glimpse in the Bible. We want to know how to live in ways that please Him and fulfill us. But more often than not, the Bible remains either an opaque witness to spiritual awareness or a book that seems completely out-of-date.

In the first volume, we looked at the significant difference in worldview between our Greek-based, Western understanding of the world and the biblical ancient near-Eastern, Semitic view of the world. Those two paradigms represent radical changes in perspective when it comes to social structures, education, relationships, public and private mores and government. Those paradigms are often obscured by translations that accommodate our Western outlook. The biblical view of how the world works and what the world is all about is fundamentally opposed to many of the standard assumptions we Westerns have about the nature of the world, of Man and of God.

In this second volume, I have collected material from *Today's Word* (the daily email editions for members of the At God's Table community) on the specific topics of idolatry in both ancient and contemporary cultures, leadership, the unity of work and worship, the biblical idea of "the Church," prayer, evangelism and the perennial misunderstanding of the relationship between Law and grace. I believe you will find these explorations enlightening, challenging and perhaps a bit upsetting, but that is the purpose of exploring in the first place.

Montverde, 2011

Table of Contents

Idolatry
The Temptations of Money, Sex and Power

The sages considered idolatry the greatest of all sins, not simply because it dishonored the one true God but also because idolatry denies God's rightful ownership of life and His authority to direct it for His purposes. Idolatry has been present ever since the serpent suggested personal choice trumped God's instructions. In one form or another, idolatry can probably be discovered behind every other sinful behavior. Perhaps that's why the first commandment of the Decalogue establishes God as the only true god.

Today we might imagine that idols have long since vanished from the superstitions and ignorance of men. After all, we don't worship golden calves or offer our children to Molech. But thinking that idolatry is simply the expression of ancient, uneducated cultures would be a tragic mistake. God-replacement is all around us. In fact, in is more sophisticated form, God-replacement has now become the avowed purpose of government. When a civilization allows its human governors to usurp the role legitimately played only by God Himself, society becomes idolatrous no matter how disdainfully it considers "primitive" Man.

Until we clearly understand the scope and depth of idolatry, we are more than likely to unintentionally participate in one of its many manifestations. Therefore, it is incumbent on followers of the King to not only explore the biblical admonitions concerning idolatry in its ancient forms but also to translated those warnings into contemporary language so that we don't find ourselves worshipping at the altars of false gods. As we look at various biblical discussions of idolatry, we will also be examining ourselves for the roots of this greatest of all sins are not found in frontal assaults from the world without but rather lurking in the seductive corners within.

1.

"Pray, then in this way:" Matthew 6:8

Homo Religiosus

Pray – "Prayer is the deepest activity of the human spirit. It satisfies the universal human yearning for direct contact with the Divine. It is found in all religions in various forms, and corresponds to a religion's understanding of God. If God is the end . . . then man *is* what his prayers are."[1]

Isn't it interesting that this quotation comes from an article about the Christian view of *Hindu* prayer? I would have thought the author would have focused on the utter folly of praying to Hindu gods. In fact, I'm not sure that praying to false gods is actually *prayer* at all. It has the outward appearance of prayer but it is idolatry. How can it still be called prayer? Is contact with the divine called prayer if the "divine" is nothing more than an idol? Would Isaiah or Jeremiah or Ezekiel consider uttering words before sticks and stones to be prayer? I doubt it. If prayer is the deepest longing to have contact with the divine, then we better be sure we are actually in communication with true divinity.

Of course, we don't have to burn incense before brass statues in order to mistake idolatry for prayer. We can also pray to the wrong god when our understanding of God makes Him into something He isn't. If we don't know who God is, do we really pray when we utter words to Him or are we just blurting out expressions to some mental concept of a false god? It seems to me that the Scriptures require us to know who He is before we can really communicate with Him. That raises some questions about naïve faith. If we

---

[1] Sunand Sumithra, *"A Christian View of Prayer and Spirituality in Hindu Thought,"*

expend effort to know God, can we really say that we pray to Him?

Wouldn't that be like saying that I talk with my wife but I never spend anytime with her? I might talk *at* my wife, but I certainly wouldn't be talking *with* her. It makes you wonder how much of what we call prayer is really just talking *at* God rather than having a conversation *with* God. I suppose we could measure the depth of our real conversation *with* God by examining how much effort we put into knowing Him. We might discover that our supposed relationship is the equivalent of text messaging God while we are busy with something else. Maybe fifteen minutes of devotional time in the morning isn't quite enough to enter into a real conversation called prayer.

Do you think that our struggles with prayer are actually a reflection of our lack of understanding of God's character and actions? Do you suppose that reading His words and examining His interactions with men would improve our ability to communicate with Him? Would your conversations with your spouse or your children improve if you put more effort into being present in their lives, sharing in their point of view, listening to what they have to say? If you wanted to improve your prayer experience and God told you to listen more intently to those who surround you, would you realize that human interaction is the practice field for conversation with God?

2.

*"I will punish her for the days of the Baals when she used to offer sacrifices to them and adorn herself with her earrings and jewelry, and follow her lovers, so that she **forgot** Me,"* declares the LORD. Hosea 2:13 NASB

Forget-Me-Not

Forgot – What's a "Forget Me Not"? Do we need a picture to remind us? If a picture is all it takes to understand God's message from Hosea, we should plant entire fields of "Forget Me Not" flowers. But we would still miss the point. Our cultural view of forgetting is basically cognitive, as if there is some mental image or fact that we no longer remember. If you forget what Forget Me Not flowers look like, a photo will *remind* you of them. But this is not the Hebraic understanding of "forget."

The Hebrew verb is *shakah* (*Shin-Kaf-Chet*). "Forgetting has the sense of not bringing into conscious thought and thus not allowing something to shape a response."[2] Notice that forgetting in Hebrew is a *deliberate act*. It's not a lapse of memory. It is an intentional exclusion of what should be considered. In other words, God indicts Israel not because Israel didn't remember Him but because the people refused to allow His presence to influence their actions. The people *erased* God's instructions from their minds. They knew what they should have done but they ignored it.

Now Hosea's words have application today. Have we forgotten YHWH in the Hebraic sense of *shakah*? In a nation that calls itself Christian, have we erased His instructions? It certainly seems so. Of course, there are many who sincerely bring His ways to mind and act upon them. But when more than eighty percent of the population claims to believe in God and nevertheless behaves as if God is deaf and mute, you have to wonder if *shakah* doesn't apply. This is not merely a matter of bad ethical choices. This is deliberate worship of the Ba'als, the false gods of power, money and sex that promise satisfaction but deliver death. *Shakah* is a sign of idolatry. It is planned disobedience.

---

[2] J. Andrew Dearman, *The Book of Hosea*, NICOT, p. 119.

There is forgiveness for unintentional sins in ignorance. There is punishment for forgetting.

3.

*"**Therefore**, see, I am alluring her, and shall lead her into the wilderness, and shall speak to her heart,* Hosea 2:14 (Institute for Scripture Research)

Non Sequitur

Therefore – Israel is a mess. God sends Hosea to pronounce His verdict. Israel has become an idolatrous, disobedient nation filled with violence, abuse and perversion (sounds like other nations, doesn't it?). Israel has not fulfilled its commission. It is not representing God's character on earth. It looks just like every other pagan nation. There is no justification and no excuse. The verdict is in. Israel will be punished.

We expect the next thing that God says to be the sentencing. But what happens next is a complete non sequitur from a human perspective. "Therefore" (*laken*), says God, "I will woo Israel back to its beginnings, to the place of My refuge, to My love and concern." What? Israel is full of prostitution, adultery, idolatry and moral failure. For this reason, God takes them back? The rationale is *completely backwards*. If anything, God should give up on this people and cast them away as a failed experiment. But that's not what happens. Dearman suggests that *laken* should be translated "even so" in this verse just to make sense of this impossible conclusion.[3] In spite of all that Israel has done, God doesn't give up. Punishment? Yes. Abandonment? Not a chance. God sees Israel's debauchery for what it really is - a cry for help. He will bring chastisement because He must get

---

[3] J. Andrew Dearman, *The Book of Hosea*, NICOT, p. 119.

Israel's attention, but because God loves Israel, He will not walk away. Israel has divorced YHWH, but YHWH has not divorced Israel.

We have a lot to learn in the book of Hosea. First we learn some very important lessons about God's faithfulness. He keeps His promises no matter what. That alone should be enough for us to raise a red flag when theologians begin to talk about a "new" Israel. If God doesn't give them up after the pronouncement of Hosea, He certainly isn't going to give them up 1,000 years later.

Second, we learn that Israel's idolatry and disobedience is exactly like ours. We chase the Ba'als just like they did. Power, money, sex and all of its variations come wooing us. Far too often we follow them. God steps in with punishment – and love. Since He doesn't give up, He views all disobedience as the opportunity to turn us around. The lesson from Hosea is that no matter how far we have fallen, the distance is never insurmountable. God's wilderness is right around the corner.

Finally, we discover that punishment is the best thing for wayward children. This is *not* wrath (make sure you know the difference). Without punishment there is no incentive to turn (*shuv*), therefore punishment is a moral imperative. When God has you under His thumb, rejoice. It is a sure sign that He is not giving up on you. He intends to bring you back and you have the stripes to prove it.

4.

With this ram the priest shall make **atonement** *before Yahweh for the sin which he has committed.* Leviticus 19:22 NASB

Koran vs. Tanakh

Atonement – Many Hebrew words have cognates (similar words) in other middle-Eastern languages. One of those languages is Arabic. So it isn't surprising to find that the Hebrew word *kaphar* has some relationship to the Arabic word *kaffara*, a word which mean "absolve." This Arabic word is borrowed from Hebrew. That might lead you to think that the idea of atonement in the Koran is the same as the idea of atonement in the Tanakh, but you would be mistaken. Knowing the difference is fundamental to understanding the enormous gap between Judaism (and Christianity) and Islam. In fact, once we understand the real difference, we see that some past forms of Christianity are far closer to Islam than the Tanakh will ever be.

Kaphar (to atone, to expiate – with some differences in the nuances, remember?) is central to the Hebrew idea of forgiveness. Essentially, atonement is an act needed to restore a relationship between two parties when that relationship has been severed through some transgression. What is crucial in the Hebraic view is that the break in the relationship is not emotional. It does not occur because of hurt feelings or social displeasure. The break is *legal*. It is *contractually based*. One party has aggrieved the other and this grievance must be repaired by some legally sufficient act. It doesn't matter which party initiates the act of atonement. It only matters that without this act the relationship cannot be restored.

In Israel, atonement is accomplished when the person who has caused the break in the relationship fulfills the restoration obligations demanded by the aggrieved party. This involved a sacrifice. The kind of grievance determined the kind of sacrifice. Atonement could be accomplished through the imposition of punishment (a thief can atone, for example, by repaying what he took plus twenty percent).

But when God was the offended party in deliberate sin, final atonement had to be accomplished by God since the penalty included the *death* of the offender. God's sacrifice is at the heart of the act of atonement.

This is not the case in Islam. Atonement in Islam is the act of a merciful god *without* the need for sacrifice. In other words, *kaffara* (Arabic) implies concealing or covering up transgression, not the removal of transgression through payment of the debt.[4] In Islam, forgiveness is a matter of white-washing the sin, not of cleansing it. The moral debt isn't erased. It is swept under the carpet. Ethical and moral balance is never achieved. Holiness is not maintained. In the end, the sin remains, but Allah *pretends* it no longer matters.

Now you can understand why Muslims are devoted practitioners of even the most violent aspects of their faith. They are never actually forgiven. They must continually

---

[4] The Arabic word is used throughout the Koran. Here are but two examples for Sura 5.

5:12 GOD had taken a covenant from the Children of Israel, and we raised among them twelve patriarchs. And GOD said, "I am with you, so long as you observe the Contact Prayers (Salat), give the obligatory charity (Zakat), and believe in My messengers and respect them, and continue to lend GOD a loan of righteousness. I will then *remit* your sins, and admit you into gardens with flowing streams. Anyone who disbelieves after this, has indeed strayed off the right path."

8:29 O ye who believe! If ye keep your duty to Allah, He will give you discrimination (between right and wrong) and will rid you of your evil thoughts and deeds, and will *forgive* you. Allah is of Infinite Bounty.

meet the obligations of Allah in order for him to not recall their transgressions. As long as they are obedient, and only as long as they are obedient, Allah will turn his wrath away. But one slip in devotion, and it all comes back. It is simply impossible for Islam to claim that Allah removes guilt as far as the East is from the West. Guilt is always there, under the prayer rug.

In past centuries some theological expression within Christianity tended to move might recall the endless process of achieving righteousness through certain Roman Catholic rituals, for example. Fortunately, none of these are part of the Hebrew concept of *kaphar*. *Kaphar* is true payment. Transgression is not concealed. It is *paid for*. It no longer applies. Raise your voices in praise to YHWH who forgives for He casts our guilt as far as the East is from the West, never again to become a burden.

5.

*On the next day Moses said to the people, "You yourselves have committed a great sin; and now I am going up to the LORD, perhaps I can **make atonement** for your sin."* Exodus 32:30 NASB

Who Will Pay?

Make atonement – God is *never* appeased! Appeasement is demanded by pagan deities, not by YHWH. Why? Because appeasement implies that the deity is in a state of wrath or anger and that some human action is needed to defer that anger. Appeasement suggests that human beings are able, through their own efforts, to assuage the anger of the gods. But the Hebrew view begins from an entirely different perspective. God isn't *angry* at us. He is brokenhearted.

God loves His creation. Our rebellion produces a broken relationship that He is anxious to restore. Of course, if all His efforts fail, the moral integrity of the creation calls for punishment, but this is not His *beginning* state of mind. That's why the Hebrew verb *kipper* "never refers to propitiation of God. Even when a human person is the subject of the action, *kipper* denotes the action of a substitutionary mediator, effecting forgiveness of sin."[5]

How is atonement made? Someone stands between the offender and the offended. Someone acts as a mediator. Someone offers payment on behalf of the offender in order to restore the relationship with the offended.

In most of the sacrificial settings, a priest acts as the mediator. The offering becomes the payment required by the offended party in order to heal the broken relationship. The Torah spells out in great detail exactly what is required to restore such broken relationships. The requirement implies a legal setting much like a court of law where certain restitution must be made to satisfy the judgment. This works perfectly when the offenses concern interactions between human beings (for example, when a man steals someone's property). Atonement is the payment of the penalty. But what happens when the offended party is God Himself? What happens when my sin breaks relationship with Him? How will I atone for that? I am the offender. I can't come to the offended one, YHWH, on my own because I am the one who broke the relationship. I need a mediator.

We see this principle in action when Israel offends YHWH in the incident of the golden calf. Moses must act as the mediator. Even with Moses in the middle, the outcome is uncertain. *"Perhaps* I can make atonement." Why isn't the

---

[5] Lang, *kipper*, TDOT, Vol. 7, p. 294

atonement guaranteed? Moses isn't certain what God will require as payment. And Moses might not be sure if God will accept his role as mediator. There is a lot at risk here since the required payment has not been specified. Moses is doing all that he knows to do and all that he can do, but it might not be enough. The price might just be too high for anyone to pay. This sin is a "great sin," a sin of blasphemy and idolatry, a sin that offends the very nature of God since it implies God is not who He claims to be. The punishment for this sin is death. But who can pay such a price? Must every one of the children of Israel die in order to balance the books? Must you and I be put to death because we too have committed a great sin?

God says, "NO!" "I will take your place." No man can ransom the life of another from God. In fact, no man is able to ransom even his own life from God (Psalm 49:8). The price exceeds our ability to pay. Who then will pay?

Only God.

And He does.

6.

*"Therefore it is my judgment that we do not trouble those who are turning to God from among the Gentiles, but that we write to them that they abstain from things **contaminated** by idols and from fornication and from what is strangled and from blood."* Acts 15:19-20 NASB

Torah Alignment

Contaminated – What's in your refrigerator? That might be the appropriate modern-day question to introduce James' pronouncement. Far too often Christian theologians have suggested that this passage eliminates all Torah requirements except the rules given to Noah. That's probably because most interpreters in the last millennium have ignored the *context* of this announcement. We will not. Let's take a longer look at what James has to say.

James is Jewish (despite the Anglicized name). He is Ya'aqob, recognized leader of the Jerusalem assembly (*qehillah*) of the followers of the Way. Everything about him stems from his Jewish roots and his understanding and worship of Yeshua *Ha-Mashiach*. When he speaks, he speaks from the authority of the Tanakh (the Hebrew Scriptures). His concern is not about how his fellow countrymen become "Christians." His concern is about all the Gentiles who are joining the Jewish *qehillah*. After listening to the discussion, he determines that only four things are really **required** of these Gentile converts. He agrees with Sha'ul that outward circumcision is not a requirement. A Gentile does not have to become a Jew (the ritual process of becoming a Jew included circumcision) in order to be a participant in the fellowship of the *qehillah*. That is settled. What a Gentile must do, however, is meet four specific requirements. These requirements begin with the idea of pagan contamination (in Greek, *alisgema*, a word occurring only here in the New Testament). Of course, Ya'aqob wasn't speaking Greek. So whatever he said must be related to a Jewish-Hebrew perspective. And once we begin to look there, we find something very interesting, not found in the Genesis account of Noah.

Whoever participates in table fellowship in the *qehillah* has fellowship with YHWH. The Tanakh makes it clear that table fellowship incorporates "clean" food and specific kosher rituals.[6]   Gentiles who are entering the *qehillah* fellowship are required to participate in the table fellowship according to Tanakh practice.   They may *not* participate in sacrificial meals to pagan deities because table fellowship was a symbol of worship.   In other words, a person could not participate in pagan rituals and, *at the same time*, participate in table fellowship with YHWH.   This requirement has nothing to do with "earning" salvation. Salvation is God's gift. But it has everything to do with living a life in honor of YHWH and participating in the community called apart by YWHW.   James effectively says, "You can't keep on doing those things associated with pagan table fellowship. You have to leave all those behind."

Now look at the four requirements.   In the *context* of the first century, Jewish culture in Jerusalem, each of these four actions would have been considered signs of pagan worship (offerings to idols, sexual worship rituals, strangulation rather than kosher slaughter, drinking blood or using blood in ways other than those prescribed by God). So James says, "None of these can be allowed," not because he is making a pronouncement about food but because these fellowship-related behaviors are associated with idolatry.

If you are going to participate at God's table, you need to give up your idolatrous ways.   Today, James might have a different list, a list that includes *our* symbols of serving other gods. Table fellowship with YHWH comes in only one flavor – His.

So, what's in your refrigerator?   And what's in your heart? Have you put aside all those actions and elements that signal idolatry in any form? Have you determined that you will sit at God's table according to His directions?   Or are you trying to eat from your own menu?

---

[6] cf. 1 Samuel 9:13, Jeremiah 11:15, Haggai 2:12, Zechariah 14:21

7.

*"Then you shall say to Pharaoh, 'Thus says the LORD, "Israel is **My son**, My firstborn."* Exodus 4:22 NASB

One of a Kind

My son – We have a tendency to believe that God often spoke of Israel as His son, but this isn't the case. In fact, there are only two places in the Tanakh where God refers to Israel as "My son." The first is here in this verse and the next. The second is in Hosea 11:1. Our mistaken conclusion about the frequency of God's description of Israel as His son probably comes from the fact that Matthew uses the Hosea passage as a Messianic prophecy (Matthew 2:15). But the truth is that this expression is quite rare. It is used in Exodus because YHWH is confronting another being who also claims to be a god, namely Pharaoh, and as we soon find out, the issue of the firstborn son becomes a critical battle line in YHWH's war against the Egyptian deities.

The Hebrew phrase, *beni Yisra'el*, tells us something crucial about Israel's place in God's creation. First, it tells us God considers Israel as the elected heir of His purposes. Second, this phrase clearly places Israel in an exclusive relationship with God as a part of God's family. In conjunction with God's declaration that Israel is His "firstborn," we realize that no other people or nation can ever occupy this place in God's heart. Many may be adopted but none except Israel can be "firstborn." When God established His covenant with Israel at Sinai, the implications stretched across the entire history of humanity. The promise to Abraham was to be fulfilled in the nation of Israel and in all those who attached themselves to that nation. That promise is still being fulfilled today.

The New Testament authors adopt this same language in reference to Yeshua. This is particularly important since the expression is used so infrequently in the Tanakh. As the New Testament authors report, Yeshua steps into the place of Israel and fulfills the commission originally intended for God's chosen people. He becomes what they refused to become – a royal priest to the nations. His mission was rehabilitation. He came to bring Israel *back* to the assignment God gave them. That's why He says He has come to the lost sheep of the house of Israel. They are lost because they don't know who they are as the ones called to open the door to the nations. They have forgotten what they were supposed to be doing. They aren't lost due to wandering away from their commitment to YHWH. Since Babylon they never went back to idolatry. They are lost because they have wandered away from their identity as priests to the nations. Yeshua restores this missing perspective. Peter acknowledges this restoration when he proclaims that the event on the temple mount (Acts 2) is a sign of God's spirit poured out on *all nations*. The door has been opened – again.

What does this mean for Gentiles, people like most of us? It means that Israel is still the firstborn son. There is no justification for saying that Israel has been replaced with some other "firstborn." That would be impossible. It also means that those who are adopted become sons with the same covenant and commission as the firstborn. The firstborn son is the model we follow – the model of Israel and subsequently, the model of Israel renewed in Yeshua. Just as Israel was commissioned to be a royal priesthood to the nations, so are all adopted sons. A priest is the intercessor between God and men, instructing men what God demands of them in order to join in fellowship at His table. And that's what we are supposed to be doing now.

In fact, if we do that according to the original commission, we Gentiles will spur those born from Abraham's lineage to recognize that the door is really open. Our actions will induce Israel to look at our claim to follow Yeshua HaMashiach as valid because we will be doing what God assigned to His son.

8.

*Beloved, do not believe every spirit, but **test** the spirits to see whether they are from God; because many false prophets have gone out into the world.* 1 John 4:1 NASB

The Great Deceiver

Test – When John wrote his letters, the messianic congregations were under attack. Buffeted between Hellenism through Gnostic and pagan religions and the Judaism that rejected Yeshua as the Messiah, the early followers of the Way had to know how to evaluate claims made by teachers. In the past, Moses provided two tests. First, if the words spoken by a man claiming to be a prophet did not come true, then that man was not from God (Deuteronomy 18:22). Second, even if the man's predictions came true, any man who led the people toward idolatry was not from God (Deuteronomy 13:1-5). Certainly John was aware of these tests, but now he adds another. Anyone who claims that Yeshua did not come in the flesh is a false prophet. John's test is aimed directly at Gnosticism and its cousin, Docetism. Today this heretical view has all but disappeared among Christians. That makes us think we have met the tests for prophets, but maybe this conclusion isn't quite right. Docetism may have disappeared, but other false teachings have taken its place.

In John's day, the teaching that Yeshua only *appeared* to be a man (but was really God disguised in human form) was a formidable Hellenistic enemy of the faith. On the opposite side was the continued battle with Judaism that Yeshua wasn't really God at all. He was just another man, certainly not the Messiah. Followers of the Way had to combat both of these opposing views. But that didn't remove the tests provided by Moses. Those were firmly established in the Torah. Today we have settled the Docetic heresy and we hope that by our way of life we will encourage Jews to recognize Yeshua as the Messiah, but we still have a problem with Moses. John's use of the verb *dokimazo* exhorts us to try, to test, to discern and distinguish those teachings that lead to idolatry and reject them and the ones who promote them. The root behind this verb is the idea of accepting what has been received and proved. You find the same thought in 2 Timothy 2:15; the man *approved* by God who needs not be ashamed. But here's the catch. What John considered accepted and proved is the Torah observance of Yeshua and the utter reliability and applicability of the Tanakh. In other words, Moses' second test validates John's claim of Yeshua's divinity and His role as the Messiah because it leads directly to a life built on the Torah. Anything else leads toward idolatry. The rejection of God's instructions for living implies the rejection of the God who gives the instructions.

Now we have an enormous problem. The Church has rejected Docetism, upholding John's test, but it fails to meet the conditions of Moses' tests. In fact, one might argue that the Church itself is the great deceiver, suggesting that it is no longer necessary to practice what God said in the Old Testament. Such a claim implies that it is no longer necessary to believe what Yeshua Himself said. Such a claim would have been idolatry for John and all followers of the Way. How we came to accept what the Church taught but reject what Scripture teaches is a very long story, but it doesn't change the situation. We have failed to test the spirits because we have rejected Moses. We threw out the tests that would have kept us on track and then claimed that we could alter Scripture to fit our own discernment. Unless we take seriously this shift in our own history, we will continue toward idolatry even when we believe the truth about Yeshua.

John wrote about those prophets who denied the human reality of Yeshua. We aren't fighting that battle. Our concern is much older. Moses wrote about those prophets who spoke true words but lead the people astray. That seems to be our fight. It's far more subtle and far more dangerous. And few there will be who find the narrow gate.

9.

And YHWH Elohim **formed** *Man out of dry, loose earth dirt*
Genesis 2:7a (my translation)

Sin Revisited (3)

Formed – "To bring desire into existence." That's *yatsar*. God desired partnership in the regulation and enhancement of His creation. That desire was manifested in the formation of Man. Because the desire to bring into existence is the essence of the image of God, Man shares this passion with the Creator. God created this passion *good*! It is not evil by itself. It is, in fact, an expression of who God is. But because it is directionless, it can be misused. The *yetzer ha'ra* is the *misuse* of divinely-installed passion. The rabbis tell us just how subtle and disguised this misuse can be. "The evil impulse is at first like a passer-by, then like a lodger, and finally like the master of the house."[7] They point out that

---

[7] Abraham Cohen, *Everyman's Talmud*, p. 91.

the reign of the evil impulse is tantamount to idolatry within. "There shall be no strange god in thee" (Psalm 81:9) is interpreted as a remark about the *yetzer ha'ra* that dwells within a man. Our job, with the help of the Lord, is to kick out the lodger and reinstall the rightful Master. This is why life on the Way is a battle, a journey fraught with danger, a walk in the valley of the shadow of death. And this is why the presence of His rod and staff comfort. Both are needed if we are to persevere. This is why initiation into His fellowship is never the end of the story. Until the last of my desire to bring into being is submitted to the Lord of life, I will be in need of assistance, reinforcements and deliverance.

Yatsar is God's verb of formation. And God makes good. Therefore, *yatsar* in my life and in yours is good. God made it so. The issue we face is not the corrupt character we inherit. It is the problem of the *choice* we make with the power to bring desire into being. In other words, the significant difference between Judaism and some Christian theology (but not all, of course) is that Judaism expresses the conviction that Man is "unfettered" is his will. "The nature of his life is molded by his desires. He *can* misuse life's opportunities if he so wishes, but in no circumstances would it be agreed that he *must* misuse them. The evil impulse constantly tempts him; but if he fall, the responsibility is his and his alone."[8]

With this in mind, we can easily see why the Bible places so much emphasis on *continuing* in the faith and, frankly, so little on the initial act of acceptance. Everywhere in Scripture we encounter encouragement and instruction to keep on track.

---

[8] Ibid., p. 95.

Everywhere we find exhortation to abide in the commandments. The contemporary emphasis on a single act of dedication or a moment's declaration of belief is absent from Scripture. What matters is what we do in the long run, one day at a time. And nothing except our own misused passionate desire can prohibit us from becoming what God formed.

10.

*For a God **jealous** (is) YHWH your God* Deuteronomy 6:15

God's Honor

Jealous – Biblical metaphors depend on the cultural behaviors and expectations of the audience. Just like the parables of Yeshua, metaphors don't make a lot of sense if they are removed from their cultural background. The description of God as *el qana' YHWH* (God jealous YHWH) might be considered incompatible with the character of the God we think we know if we don't understand the biblical background of jealousy.

In our culture, jealousy is not a positive attribute. In fact, we might even consider it a sin. Consequently, we have a hard time understanding how God can say, "I am a jealous God." Our understanding of jealousy has been subjected to psychological therapy. We seek the balanced emotional life of "respect" for others. We try to repress those burning feelings that come from relationship betrayal because we have been taught that only positive emotions are healthy. But this is not the biblical picture. God's relationship to His people is a relationship of intimacy, fidelity and unwavering commitment, usually on His behalf alone. A breach of that relationship is an attack on God's honor, just as a rival for the love of my spouse is an attack on my honor. The metaphor is based in sexual exclusivity. Marital fidelity means ownership. You belong to me. I belong to you. The covenant bond is exhibited in sexual union. Anyone who attempts to break this bond of mutual ownership insults the owner. In a culture where personal and public honor are more important than life itself, such a usurper must be resisted in every possible way. To allow a rival is to relinquish my dignity.

God is jealous because He will never allow anyone or anything to put Him in second place with the ones He loves. He will countenance no rival for His affections. He will resist any attempt to breach the intimacy He offers to His bride. He will never let His honor be diminished by some act or actor. He is deadly serious about His love for us. That's why the metaphors for idolatry are so often sexual. No self-respecting person allows his or her lover to be shared with another!

Since we know how God feels about this situation, the next question is this: Who would dare break such a bond? Who would risk the reprisals of God to defense of His honor? Actually, we don't have to look very far to discover the perpetrator. It is us. God never leaves His people, but His people attempt to divorce Him. Hosea is a living picture of the intense emotional struggle of God in His effort to restore His honor and recapture the love of His people. We are the culprits here. Israel's history of adultery is our legacy – if we don't learn from their lessons. We only need to fear ourselves and our temptations to chase another lover. May it never be! May each of us rest in His intimate concern. May we open our arms to the One who would love us eternally. God's jealousy is our greatest protection. Embrace it because it is the sign of His faithfulness.

11.

*You shall not **test** YHWH your Elohim as you tested In Massah.*
Deuteronomy 6:16

History Lesson

Test – God *commands* us not to test Him. Hmm. What do you suppose that means? Am I not to doubt? Am I not to question? Am I not to ask? I won't be able to answer these questions unless I know the story of Massah. I need *history* to worship properly. I am never removed from the connection to the people who came before me.

What happened at Massah fills in the context of the Hebrew verb *nasah* (to test, to try, to prove). This verb is used to describe God's tests of faithfulness (cf. Genesis 22), so it isn't always a
disapproved action. But something happened at Massah that should never be repeated. Often the text of the story circulates around the word "quarrel." But this isn't strong enough. At Massah the people *accused* Moses and God of impotence and indifference. They said, "If You don't take care of us as we expect, God, we are not going to follow You any more. You have to *prove* that You are God and that you care for us!" In other words, they challenged God's power and His benevolence in spite of ample evidence to the contrary. Why did they do this? Because they believe God should act according to *their* will. They demonstrated that their faith depended entirely on what God would *do* for them, not on who God was. They questioned God's promise of providential care, relegating Him to the role of a wish-fulfilling genie.

God will not be insulted. Neither will He allow men to dictate how He cares for His people. He is not under our control and we do not tell Him what is good. The test at

Massah is a sign of rebellious disobedience, a refusal to accept the character of God as the basis of obedience. At Massah, the Israelites decided they would rather be in Missouri ("I'll believe it when I see it"). God was not pleased.

What do we learn from this history lesson? First, we learn that the theme of rebellious disobedience in the face of overwhelming evidence of God's goodness is sin. God cares. How His care is manifest in our lives is *not* our concern. That He cares is all we need to know. We are His servants, not His board of directors. Whenever we begin to think that we are due some consideration from the Most High, we need to remember Massah.

Second, we learn that any action questioning the providential care of God is dangerous. Faith cannot be based on my perception of how God meets my needs. That is not faith. That is presumptive idolatry. If my believing depends on God doing what I think He needs to do for me, I am no different than the man who trusts in his money to feed him, his insurance to protect him and his lovers to satisfy him. God is God without any requirement to act at all. That He acts on my behalf only demonstrates His faithfulness. Gratitude is the basis of faith, but gratitude arises from who He is, not what He does.

Third, we may begin to see that Yeshua didn't die for *my* sins. He died for the love of the Father. Forgiveness is the by-product of Yeshua's obedience. Yeshua went to the cross because He trusted the character of the Father. The Father tested Yeshua's faith and found him worthy. May that also be true of us.

12.

Therefore, we are ambassadors for Christ, as though God were *entreating through us; we beg you on behalf of Christ, **be reconciled** to God.* 2 Corinthians 5:20

Marriage Counseling

Be Reconciled – By now we have learned that God's covenant relationship with us is reflected in the metaphor of marital faithfulness. It's not just about sexual fidelity but sex has a very big role to play in this metaphor, so much so that idolatry is viewed in sexual terms. Just in case we thought that Paul wasn't Jewish, he reminds us of his deep understanding of the Jewish marriage metaphor by choosing the Greek term *katallasso* as the verb about returning to the Lord.

Katallasso means "to reconcile," but it doesn't mean to come to a mental understanding of correct belief. In fact, this verb is used in 1 Corinthians 7:11 about marriage reconciliation. This Greek verb is the verb for marriage counseling. It is the goal and the means by which estranged couples reunite. And if Paul uses this
verb as the actions required of broken marriages, how much
more applicable is it when it comes to broken fellowship with the Great Lover.

Using *katallasso* has some interesting implications. First, no one can be reconciled unless a relationship *previously* existed and is now broken. We don't tell strangers to be reconciled because they have never had a relationship with each other. We encourage them to *begin* being friends, not to become friends again. Paul's use of this term implies that his readers *had a prior* relationship with God and that relationship has been broken because of their infidelity. This certainly puts a kink in the application of this verse to pagan evangelism. Is Paul suggesting that those who never knew God need to be *reconciled*, or is he saying that there are readers of this letter who once were part of the fellowship of followers but have fallen away?

Second, Paul's use of *katallasso* parallels the Hebrew Scripture's use of *shuv*. God is constantly and consistently calling Israel to *return* (*shuv*) to Him, to be reconciled to Him and restored to His purpose. But God doesn't call the pagan nations to return. They can't return. They were never with Him to begin with. Pagans *convert*. Jews *return*. When Paul uses this parallel Greek verb, he implies that his audience consists of those who were once at home with God. They are not pagans. They are God's *divorced and estranged* people. When you think about the issues Paul addresses in his letter to Corinth, this should not be surprising. The Messianic community in Corinth was in serious trouble, not because they didn't know the one true God, but because their behavior was completely inconsistent with living according to God's directions. They were traitors to God's government and adulterers to God's covenant. No wonder they needed reconciliation.

In the end, we discover that Paul is reaching out to those who were once part of the fellowship but now don't *live like it*. Their error is not believing in false gods. Their error is divorcing God. They knew the joy of His bond, but they chose to live for their own agendas. Perhaps there are a lot more who need to be reconciled than we thought. Perhaps the most important function of the "church" is divorce counseling with those who thought marriage to God only meant signing the contract.

13.

*All things are **lawful** for me, but not all things are profitable. All things are lawful for me, but I will not be mastered by anything.* 1 Corinthians 6:12

Missing Punctuation

Lawful – Brian Rosner makes an off-hand remark about this passage that deserves considerably more attention. He says, "Apparently some Corinthians were eating in pagan temples and using the prostitutes on offer on such occasions and defending both behaviors with the slogan, 'all things are lawful for me'."[9]   Rosner is the senior lecturer in New Testament at Moore Theological College.   He is a well-respected scholar.   What he says here is startling.   This remark catches us off-guard because it alters completely the context of Paul's statement.   What it suggests is that Paul really needed to add some quotation marks.   Of course, those aren't available in Greek so sometimes, but not always, Paul indicates that he is citing a straw man or his opponents or someone else.   But on some occasions Paul doesn't bother to tell us who is speaking.   Since he is writing to people who would *know* what was said, he simply repeats the comment.   These occasions are the most perplexing.   That's when we have to rely on the context.

We know that this occurs because we find the same citation without quotation marks in Galatians when the text concerning the silence of women says, "as the law says." But, of course, the law doesn't say this.   It can't be found *anywhere* in Hebrew Scriptures.   So, obviously, Paul is not telling us that this is what he thinks.   He is citing his detractors. We're just missing the quotation marks.

Rosner's point is that Paul's context here is all about members of the assembly who are still incorporating

---

[9] Brian Rosner, *Greed as Idolatry*, p. 114.

common pagan practices into their lives. Paul has just referred to these pagan practices, among which were temple prostitution and pagan festivals (which were usually an excuse for orgies). What Rosner suggests is that this famous phrase, "All things are lawful for me," is *not* Paul's words but rather the words of those he is debating.

Oh, my! Take a deep breath. Recall the agonizing theological machinations we all went through while we tried to explain these words within the context of a Torah-observant morality, or even within the higher ethical expectations of Christian holiness. Remember how difficult it was to walk the razor's edge between moral imperatives and ethical choice. Imagine how that would have changed if we just added the quotation marks.

Rosner's comment makes a lot of sense. Paul is Torah-observant. He says so. Torah observance does *not* make all things lawful. In fact, there are a lot of things that are expressly forbidden. Changing the translation to "all things possible" doesn't help much. While the Greek verb, *exesti*, can be translated "what is possible," the implication is morally or legally possible or permitted. But clearly not all things are permitted, morally possible or endorsed by the Torah. The only way we can make sense of this statement *as Paul's own words* is to claim that Paul adopted a view of grace that set aside *all* the requirements of the Torah and therefore, the Torah no longer instructed him. But this is impossible. Paul never set aside the Torah. It was his guide to every facet of life. As Heschel would say, "A Jew without Torah is obsolete." And Paul was certainly a Jew.

This means that the words, "all things are permitted, lawful, possible" makes no sense whatsoever as Paul's view of the world. These are words that describe that man who wishes an excuse for his behavior.

All we needed were the quotation marks.

Do you feel better now?

13.

*saying, "Woe, woe, the great city, she who was **clothed** in fine linen and purple and scarlet, and adorned with gold and precious stones and pearls;"* Revelation 18:16

Greed In Disguise

Clothed – You're reading John's apocalyptic revelation. You know that apocalyptic literature is filled with symbols and literary allusions. You're Jewish. You know your own Scriptures because you have heard them read to you since you were a child. Then you come across this verse. What do you think about it?

For most of us, this is just a description of the royal clothing, the luxury, of the symbol of idolatry and disobedience – Babylon. We don't connect this with other passages in Scripture because we don't have that rich history of the Jewish culture. But John did. He wasn't writing to Western Europeans or Americans. He was writing to Messianic Jews. When he used the words *'ei peribebliemenei bussinon kai porphuroun kai kokkinon* (clothed

in fine linen and purple and scarlet), his reading audience would think of Exodus 28:5 (and 15-17), *ve-et- hatchelet ve-et-haargaman ve-et-tolaat*. Fine linen, purple and scarlet had a very special use in Exodus. These were the material of the robes of the High Priest.

Suddenly we see that John's revelation connects disobedience and idolatry to an imitation of true worship.

Every reader in John's culture would have recognized that the clothing of Babylon was a mockery of God's adornment of His priest. The Great Whore mimics God's anointed. The characteristics of Babylon might *appear* to be religious, but the truth is quite the opposite.

What do we learn from John's deliberate connection between God's adornment and the false counterpart? What we learn is that the other characteristics of Babylon are also imitations of God's Kingdom. The copy looks right but it is corrupt to the core. And what does that copy look like? Well, we might start with Babylon's promotion of luxury. In a word, this is the idolatry of greed. Heschel helps us see the compelling power of this god. "Judaism is spiritual effrontery. The tragedy is that there is disease and starvation all over the world, and we are building more luxurious hotels in Las Vegas. Social dynamics are no substitute for moral responsibility. The most urgent task is to destroy the myth that accumulation of wealth and the achievement of comfort are the chief vocations of man."[10]

Babylon didn't disappear in the 7th Century BC. Babylon is here today. Greed is the god of this age, and of many ages in the history of Man. Greed isn't limited to the millionaire who wants "just one more." Greed is the desire to have according to *my* expectations, without consideration for God's purposes.

So the men of Israel took some of their provisions, and did not ask for the counsel of the LORD. Joshua 9:14

"Do not work for the food which perishes, but for the food which endures to eternal life, which the Son of Man will give to you, for on Him the Father, God, has set His seal." John 6:27

---

[10] Abraham Heschel, *Moral Grandeur and Spiritual Audacity*, p. 31.

14.

*I showed you all these things, that working in this way we ought to help those being weak, and remember the words of the Lord Jesus, that He said, "It is more blessed to give than **to receive**."* Acts 20:35

Contradiction

To Receive – Read the words of Yeshua cited by Paul. Do they really make any sense? Think about it. Does Yeshua really compare the *blessing* of giving with the *blessing* of receiving, and then tell us that one blessing is better than the other? Is there something *wrong* with receiving? Is receiving a lesser spiritual action than giving? I should hope not! Where would any of us be if *receiving* from the Lord carried less of a blessing than the Lord's giving? We've read these words (and probably said them) so often that we never stop to think about what they imply. But a look at the Greek text indicates that maybe we don't have this translation quite right, and when we really understand what Yeshua said, everything changes.

The Greek verb here is *lambano*. It can mean "receive" but it also means "to take hold of, to seize, to actively take." While the statement sounds so spiritual in its traditional form, the context doesn't support such a reading. Paul is talking about his selfless actions on behalf of the congregation at Ephesus. He specifically mentions the fact that he did not take anything for himself. He says that he even supported himself during the ministry in Ephesus. In other words, he was a living example of giving *without taking*. Reading his quotation of Yeshua as though it means *receiving* doesn't fit the context. Paul did receive from the people at Ephesus. He belonged to that community. He shared in their meals, their worship, their fellowship and their lives. But he didn't use his position for accumulation. Instead of building up his own storehouse, he *gave* back. "It is more blessed to give than to accumulate – to take hold or seize."

How would our behavior have to change if Yeshua told us that giving is the antidote to amassing wealth? Clearly the behavior of the early Messianic congregations demonstrates the actions of giving rather than accumulating. In fact, there are many occasions in Scripture where we are exhorted to use what God graciously provides for the benefit of others. This is one of the great contradictions of faith. Our lives are not measured by how much we collect or acquire or control. Our lives are measured by how much we *distribute* from what God provides. We are the pipelines of His grace for others, and that includes physical resources.

Brian Rosner makes this point: " . . . the greedy are those with a strong desire to acquire and keep for themselves more and more money and possessions, because they love, trust and obey wealth rather than God."[11] In other words, greed is idolatry. But greed is not limited to millionaires and Wall Street bankers. Greed fits *anyone* who desires to accumulate and control. Maybe that's why it is such a dangerous component of false worship.

15.

*"For you shall not **worship** any other god, for YHWH, whose name is Jealous, is a jealous God."* Exodus 34:14

A Revelation of Worship

Worship – In order to avoid idolatry, we must know what it

---

[11] Brian Rosner, *Greed as Idolatry: The Origin and Meaning of a Paulihe Metaphor*, p. 129

means to worship. This might seem like a fairly simple thing, but we soon discover that it isn't. One problem is our rationality paradigm. In this Greek-based culture, the question of idolatry has been limited to the proper *object* of worship. We think that as long as we are worshipping the one true God rather than some false god we are worshipping properly. We think that as long as we are worshipping the one true God it no longer matters *how* we worship. We are free to express our religious devotion to God by whatever means we wish, just as long as the *object* of our worship is the right God.

But this fixation on the philosophical issue of the correct God bypasses another Hebrew concern. From the Hebraic perspective, no worship is proper worship unless it is in accordance with God's instructions for worshipping Him. And His revelation is the only way we can know what proper worship is. In other words, we are *not* free to make up any approach we wish to worship. We must worship *as He specifies*. Anything else, even if is directed toward the one true God, is still idolatry. In Hebrew, it is not simply the *object* of worship. It is also the *method* of worship.

The Hebrew verb, *shachah*, means "to bow down, to prostrate oneself." It is universally regarded as a sign of worship. But I don't recall ever being in a church service where the congregation was prostrate on the floor. We rarely even bend the knees. Why? No modern believer intends to be idolatrous. But almost all modern believers have accommodated themselves to the Greek-based rationality paradigm. Without realizing it, they have drifted toward a cognitive and intellectual view of idolatry. They don't pay any attention to the method of worship that God reveals to His people because, as far as they are concerned, they are worshipping the *correct* God. So, as you attend one church after another, you will find a wide variety of worship expressions. You will discover that worship as we know it is the invention of human minds. From choreographed stage performance to well-crafted sermons, from stirring anthems to rocked-out decibels, today's worship format is the product of centuries of tradition and innovation. But it barely resembles the instructions given by the God who is worshipped. Have you ever wondered why?

Because we accept the philosophical approach to the question of God, we no longer consider the fundamental concern, "What does God demand of me?" when it comes to worship. But worship isn't for us. It is for God. How can we worship Him if we are the ones making up the program? Do we make up the commandments and instructions in the rest of our lives? Don't you suppose that God intended us to follow His directions in honoring Him too?

16.

*"Sirs, what must I **do** to be saved?"* Acts 16:30

Driftin' Blues

Do – "The ordinary believer is not necessarily someone who has made a major decision, but rather someone who continues the tradition of his ancestors, perhaps by merely drifting or wandering about. . . . The moral argument against such a person is that he ought to be conscious of those of his actions and considerations that are of great importance for his life. Drift may be considered an extenuating circumstance in the case of great error, but it does not exonerate the person from blame."[12]

Notice the cry of the jailer. "What must I *do*?" This is a

---

[12] Halbertal and Margalit, *Idolatry*, pp. 169-170.

defining moment in his life. He must take action. He must change course. The past no longer matters. The traditions of his predecessors are useless. Now, at this moment, he must know the truth!

Ti me dei poiein says the jailer. Notice that he does not ask what he must believe. He focuses his attention on action. The two crucial Greek words, *dei* and *poieo*, carry the message, "I *must* take *action*, but I don't know what action to take." In this moment of crisis, everything he once assumed to be true about his life and his way of living has been called into question. There is no way back. What he requires is the proper steps forward.

Because Paul answers "Believe on the Lord Jesus Christ" in our translations, we automatically shift the message from action to thought. We interpret Paul as if he were providing a "salvation message" about changing one's mind. Our view of "believe" has been altered to fit the predominately rational model of religion, so we naturally assume that Paul is asking the jailer to acknowledge some truth about Jesus. But "believe on" in Paul's world has very little to do with a shift in thinking. Paul uses these Greek words as if they were the equivalent of the Hebrew *'aman* (e.g. Genesis 15:6). The principle meaning of *'aman* is not what I think. It is what I *stand on*. *'aman* is a word about foundations; what is reliable, what is firm, what is trustworthy. To believe on Yeshua HaMashiach is to adopt His words and His actions as the foundation of my words and my actions. It is to *copy* Him as a reliable and trustworthy guide for living. I may have to change my thinking in the process, but I will certainly have to change my *doing*. This is a moment when drift no longer governs my behavior. I *decide* to change the bedrock of my life, and that implies a major shift in behavior.

35

Since contemporary evangelical religion emphasizes this moment of decision, many believers can point to a change-of-direction conversion experience. But that isn't what Paul means either. To shift the bedrock of my life is to shift everything about how I subsequently behave. I move house! I don't simply decide to move house and then stay where I am while I make plans to someday change locations or wait for the moving van to arrive. The jailer knew that his way of life had to change. He could no longer drift. He needed a new course, and he needed it now.

To drift is to put more importance on the beliefs of our heritage than on the truth. To drift is to stop asking, "What must I do?"

17.

*For you have said in your heart, "I will go up to the heavens. I will raise my throne above the stars of God, and I will sit in the mount of meeting, in the side of the north. I will rise over the heights of the clouds; I will be **compared** to the Most High."* Isaiah 14:13-14

Political Idolatry

Compared – Isaiah speaks about the attitudes of Babylon. Isaiah's condemnation reveals the hubris of Babylon and Babylon's attempt to usurp the place of God in the affairs of men. Don't read this too quickly. There is something here that is very familiar, perhaps far too familiar. But we need to take a step backward in order to see the application of Isaiah's proclamation.

We need to notice that Isaiah condemns the *political* idolatry of Babylon. What is political idolatry? It is the assumption of roles and rituals by the State that rightly belong only to God. In the Hebrew worldview, only God is

King. He may grant others the permission to act as His representatives (earthly kings), but He is Lord of all creation. Any attempt by any person or power to displace His ultimate authority over *all* the affairs of men is a despicable sin because it is *war* against God's reign and rule. Babylon epitomizes this arrogant attempted *coup d'etat* by claiming that it is entitled to the highest throne. What does that mean for Babylon's citizenry?

When the State commits idolatry, it generally assumes roles that stretch beyond the political bounds. In other words, the State begins to think and act like it is God. It begins telling its citizens how they should conduct their ordinary affairs. It starts regulating all economic transactions. It takes control of education. It provides alternative "religious" practices designed to glorify the State. It demands deification of the nation and the leaders of the nation. It grasps for more and more power. It seeks control wherever possible. It determines what is justice. It decides what is good. Each of these behaviors are direct confrontations with the authority of God, for He alone is the Lawgiver over life. Whenever the State ceases to act as the Lord's servant, whenever the State rejects or ignores the strict limitations placed upon it by biblical authority, it acts idolatrously. Babylon is but one historical example of a constant threat to the sovereignty of YHWH by men who believe themselves worthy of worship. A State that assumes the role of regulator, economic engine, educator, judge, jury, provider, protector and possessor is a political entity at war with God.

In this kind of war, there are no non-combatants. As citizens of the State, we become endorsers of its unholy program whenever we adopt its offer to replace the roles rightfully belonging to God. The State is not my mother, father and brother. It is not my provider, promoter or priest. It must never become my hope, my only help or my highest good. If I allow any of these roles to become functions of the State, I mount the tower of Babel with the rest of the insurgents.

The Hebrew verb *damah* means "to make oneself like, to resemble." The pictograph, "behold, the door of chaos," is an apt image. It is possible to make an image of God without producing a single artifact. All that is needed is to usurp His role. All that is necessary is to attempt to replace Him.

18.

*to the **church** of God which is at Corinth, to those who have been sanctified in Christ Jesus, saints by calling, with all who in every place call upon the name of our Lord Jesus Christ, their Lord and ours:* 1 Corinthians 1:2

Corinthian Crazies

Church – We all know about the Corinthians. They were a mess. Internal factions. Sexual issues. Gender complaints. Difficulties with Torah observance. Accommodations with idolatry. When Paul wrote to these "saints," there were a lot of ungodly behaviors within the community. If their actions weren't so familiar, we might even suggest that they weren't really a church at all. But when we look around, we find most of the same behaviors among our own versions of church. So what Paul says to these people is probably good for us too. And Paul starts by calling them a church.

The Greek is *ekklesia*, but Paul isn't thinking about the Greek meaning of *ekklesia*. Some years ago we examined the relationship between *ekklesia* and *qahal*, one of the Hebrew words for "assembly." What we discovered is that Paul is writing to a synagogue; a synagogue that is now filling up with pagan converts and Messianic Jews. Conflict was inevitable. Perhaps that's the opening lesson about assemblies. Not everyone agrees. But Paul is not concerned with disagreement. Disagreement is healthy. In fact, it is the centerpiece of the Jewish education in Torah. Paul is concerned with destructive behavior, not discussion over words. We must be tolerant of disputes over the nuances of interpretation, but we must be intolerant of actions that threaten communal unity. Just like Torah has a hierarchy of values, so does community. And one of the highest values is reflection of the character of God in the lives of the members.

We learn something else from Paul's designation that this motley crew of believers is still a *qahal*. What two factors make them a *qahal*? The first is that they assemble to worship the King. This is the human component, manifest in action. But the second factor is that they have been called. In fact, according to Paul, they have *all* been called, even the ones who are now causing so much dissention. This is also an important lesson about the "church." Somehow or other, God had a hand in everyone who shows up. That's incredibly important. If God weren't behind the scenes, calling the ones who arrive, then we would certainly throw the rebels out. But God is behind the scenes, so we must proceed with great caution and compassion, which is exactly what Paul does. He isn't "tolerant" of destructive behavior, but he never forgets that he is dealing with God's chosen.

There are more implications about *ekklesia* as *qahal*. How does your conception of church change if you realize Paul dealt almost exclusively with synagogues. Jews and Gentiles mixed together did not pursue a multi-cultural objectives. The only goal was conforming to the Word of God, the Tanakh. But maybe these two lessons from the word "church" need to come first. Conflict and compassion go hand in hand.

19.

*Grace to you and peace from God **our Father** and the Lord Yeshua HaMashiach.* 1 Corinthians 1:3

All In The Family

Our Father – Paul has just declared Yeshua to be God (verse 2). But without taking a breath, he immediately offers a salutation from "God our Father *and* the Lord Yeshua HaMashiach." He doesn't flinch. He doesn't backpedal. He calmly asserts that God is our Father and Yeshua is the Lord, the one we call upon. It is a great mystery indeed!

At one time Christian theologians espoused the position that Jews did not speak of God as Father. In an attempt to demonstrate Yeshua broke from Jewish tradition, even men as famous as Joachim Jeremias claimed that "our Father" was unique to Jesus. Of course, now we know better. Yeshua was Jewish and so was His language. Even this little phrase connects Him to His culture and ancestry.

But Paul's point isn't about the history of this concept. Paul has another concern in mind. The Corinthian synagogue is filled with Gentiles and Jews, but God is the Father of all. In the Body, there is no difference. Every man and every woman has exactly the same family relationship to God – and consequently to each other. This is an important lesson for the Corinthians. In an assembly where some claimed superiority, Paul drives home the real distinguishing characteristic. Everyone here is part of the same family. The only strangers are the ones who have not yet come into the congregation. If everyone here is brother or sister, why are you attempting to create a hierarchy of relationship importance? How can some of you claim to be super-family members? All of us here are brothers of sisters.

We might not live in the rough and tumble world of idolatrous Corinth (we have our own versions of idolatry and debauchery), but we often share the same superiority problem that faced the Corinthian congregation. Some of us seem to feel we are "called" to be important. We are the *leaders*. We are the *elders*. We are the *bishops* and the *pastors*. Ah, but Paul reminds us that we are not more than brothers and sisters. Any *role* we play is nothing but a temporary job assignment. It is not a measure of personal status. If God calls some to be taxi drivers, accountants, landscapers or foundation directors, each and every one is just brother or sister to the rest. Jobs do not make the man.

There is a lot of misunderstanding about the difference between roles and relationships. I am quite sure that you have been exposed to the hierarchical concept of "offices" in the church. Hmm? Where did that come from? Do you think Paul placed any superiority on such job assignments? The man who speaks about feet and hands, eyes and ears can hardly be the man who proposed that some "parts" of the Body are more important than others. Brothers and sisters, we have one Father and He speaks grace and peace to all of us.

20.

O Israel, you are destroyed, but your **help** *is in Me!* Hosea 13:9

The Man With The Gun

Help – One of the most important themes of Scripture is the sovereignty over the history of men. This is a significant part of the Exodus drama. The prophets consistently proclaim God's total control of the affairs of all men, righteous or wicked. Of course, this does not mean that the Scriptures relieve men of culpability for choices. This only means that God has the last word about everything. When God declares that Israel is destroyed, He sets aside Israel's reliance on treaties, weapons or even temple rituals. Israel's disobedience brings destruction. The problem is not negotiated alliances. The problem is idolatry. The rot is from within. Stop looking to other nations, other alignments, other sources of strength or security. YHWH is Israel's help.

Before we reflect on the implications of YHWH's declaration, let's take a look at the noun He employs. The Hebrew is *ve'ezreka*, from the root verb *'azar*. There is quite a bit of difficulty about how to translate this phrase. Some contend it means something like "you are helpless without Me;" some suggest "Who is there to help you?" and some (like the NASB above) see the phrase as a statement, not a question. Regardless of the syntax, the root verb is always *'azar*. Without God, Israel is defenseless. He is help (in fact, the copula "is" does not appear in the phrase).[13]

'azar is the verb behind *'ezer*, a word that describes God's multi-faceted relationship with Israel. What functions does God perform as the *'ezer* of Israel? Exodus 18:4 – God delivers from the hand of the oppressor. He rescues from danger. Deuteronomy 33:7 – God assists, supports and reinforces Israel against her enemies. Psalm 33:20 – God is our shield, delivering us from death and showering us with lovingkindness (*hesed* – a much bigger concept than this single word can convey). Psalm 70:5 – God provides in times of affliction and need. Psalm 115:9 – God is the one

---

[13] Since there is a direct link between *'azar* and God's design of the *'ezer* (the woman), I wonder what would happen to most marriages if husbands thought of their wives in this same way. She = help.

42

that Israel must trust (see also Psalm 115:11). Psalm 146:5 – When God is *'ezer*, Israel is blessed and has hope.

The various expressions from the root word include military aid, social and moral support, deliverance, salvation, enclosure (protection) and general assistance. What is most revealing is this: God is always the assumed source of true help. For this reason, the noun *'ezer* is often used to describe the character of God. He is the *helper* par excellence. *'Azar* means "to rescue or save or to excuse." The general sense is military assistance. In contrast to the gods of idolatry, it is God's nature to help. You don't have to convince Him, appease Him, placate Him or prove your worthiness in order for Him to act on your behalf. Aside from the fact that false gods are *false*, the distinctive difference between YHWH and idols is this: God helps *in spite of our unworthiness*. God showered His love on us when we were still acting as His enemies. He helps when we least deserve it.

Israel failed to realize that YHWH offered help even when they didn't deserve it. Consequently, by refusing the offer of grace without pre-requisites, they destroyed themselves.

Now we know how to apply this most difficult Hebrew verse. YHWH is still Israel's help. That will never change. Those who are grafted into the commonwealth of Israel inherit the great *'ezer*. He stands ready. The only question is this: are we ready to receive His help, or do we still think we need to find other sources of rescue?

Oh, yes. "The Man With The Gun." The pictograph of *'azar* is "to see, weapon, person." In Hosea's world, God arrived with a sword. In our world, God carries a very big gun. He protects His own. But maybe there's another picture here too. If YHWH is my helper, maybe others see me walking with the man with the gun.

21.

*But King David said to Ornan, "No, but I will surely buy it for the full price; for I will not take what is yours for YHWH, or offer a burnt offering which **costs me nothing**."* 1 Chronicles 21:24

Market Value

Costs Me Nothing – Nancy Pearcey makes an astounding application of David's principle. She says, "The application to our own day is that we cannot 'take for the Lord' work done by another person. Nor can we make an offering that 'costs me nothing.'"[14] The Hebrew word is _ḥinnam_, a word that essentially means *gratis*. David recognizes that true worship has a cost and that cost must be mine alone. My offering means nothing to me or to God if I didn't pay the price for it.

Let's consider some practical circumstances where this biblical principle should be applied. I remember going to church as a child. My parents gave me money to put into the offering plate. It wasn't my money. It didn't come from my allowance. It taught me that the offering I gave came from someone else's effort. While I am quite sure that my parents' motivation was to demonstrate the need for tithing, the real lesson was that tithing didn't cost.

Some months ago someone notified me that a newspaper was using my work with someone else's name attached to it. Besides the fact that this is plagiarism, the offering this person made to his community was actually a sin. It cost him nothing to take what I wrote and use it "for the Lord" as

---

[14] Nancy Pearcey, *Total Truth*, p. 374.

it if were his. He needs to talk to David.

I often hear the objection, "You should give away everything you write. After all, salvation was free. Freely you have received, freely give." I think this misses the point. My rescue was *enormously* expensive. It required terrible sacrifices, from the first death to clothe my ancestors to the last death on the cross to bring me home. I received the benefit without paying the death penalty, but that did not make it free. Because my deliverance was so expensive, my offering should reflect that expense. Nothing is free. Even a gift must be purchased by someone.

Now a personal application. In the last two years I have appealed to you for support. God has been pressing me on this decision. I realize that I should have left it in His hands. I work for an audience of One and my offering to Him must come at cost to me if it is to be worthy. My appeal attempted to defer that cost and make some of it your burden. I repent for this lack of trust in the sovereignty of God. Please forgive me. If any one feels as if I have taken what was yours, I stand ready to return it to you.

David knew that worship must cost us. That's what makes it so wonderful. What does not come from my effort or my assets has little value. When I give what I earned, the sting is replaced by joy. Both feelings are important to God.

22.

*When YHWH first spoke through Hosea, YHWH said to Hosea, "Go, take to yourself a **wife of harlotry**, and have children of harlotry; . . ."* Hosea 1:2

Under The Covers

Wife of Harlotry – Did God really tell Hosea to go find a prostitute to marry? That's what the translation suggests and that is what most of us believe. But neither the text nor Hosea's emotions toward Gomer suggest such a reading. Something else is happening here that changes the story.

First, we must take account of the fact that Hosea truly *loves* Gomer. In fact, he expresses not only deep and intimate concern for her, he also indicates a strong sexual desire toward her. Nothing new here. A man in love always finds the object of his affections enticing. But under the covers there was another side to Gomer and that is the real story in this relationship.

The Hebrew terms used to describe "a wife of harlotry" are *'esheth zenunim*. This does not describe a prostitute. That would be *'ishah zonah*. In fact, searching for *'esheth* in combination with a descriptive adjective takes us to Proverbs 31:10, Ruth 3:11, Judges 5 and 2 Samuel 18. These women are valiant and vibrant examples of faith. So what happened to Gomer? The word *zenunim* is connected with adultery and idolatry. It is most often used to describe Israel's unfaithfulness. It suggests that Gomer had a hidden propensity when she married Hosea. She desired other men. She wanted to participate in fertility cult practices. Under the covers, she wanted more and more is usually easy to find. The story of Hosea is not the story of a man who loves a prostitute. It is the story of a man who marries a woman only to discover later that she changes. She *becomes* an unfaithful wife. She *becomes* a prostitute. The desire was there from the beginning but Gomer did not reign in her desire. She explored that inner craving and it took over her life. Hosea is a man who discovers too late that there was something hidden behind her attractiveness. She was a woman without moral control.

46

Now the story of Hosea becomes a much more powerful analogy of God's relationship to Israel. God didn't choose an idolatrous people. He didn't enter into a covenant with those who already were intimate with other gods. But Israel had a craving. Israel was surrounded by temptation, by permissiveness, by seduction. Fertility cults littered the landscape. God knew their weakness. That's why He commanded that *all* the artifacts of such a lifestyle be destroyed. Israel didn't listen. Israel did what Gomer did. She followed her desires. God and Hosea both knew the humiliation and the agony of betrayal. But it didn't begin that way. It began with hope and care. God and Hosea continued to hope and to care, and eventually Israel and Gomer came back. God tells Hosea about Gomer's secret. He doesn't enter the relationship blinded by love. Hosea is obedient, but it still hurts. Sometimes desires are hidden that could lead to destruction. Are we willing to look? Are we willing to reign them in?

23.

*And the Angel of YHWH **appeared** to him in the flame of fire from the middle of a thorn bush.* Exodus 3:2

Primaries

Appeared – Do you practice reading the Scriptures with an Hebraic worldview? Once the dawning occurs, and we realize that God chose Hebrew on purpose, then we will want to read the text as participants in the Hebrew culture, the ancient biblical culture. That might seem to be a simple, straightforward assignment. Just *translate* our English words into Hebrew thought, right? Just go backwards from the concepts that we employ to recover the ideas that Hebrews used to think about the world. Ah, if it were only that easy.

You see, much of the way we conceptualize the world has been so affected by the Western Greek penchant for precision, certainty and numerical reduction that we no longer *imagine* a world that isn't made up of causal connections, essential

properties and unifying theories. In other words, even our attempts to translate backwards often carry along conceptualizations that would not make sense to a Hebrew. Consider this:

"The question of why God revealed himself in the bush is not a question of how such a revelation is metaphysically possible, that is, how a nonmaterial being can embody himself in the material. Rather, the question is why the king of kings chose to reveal himself precisely from such a lowly object as bush."[15] Once again we are reminded that in our world the primary question is "How?" but in the world of the Hebrew the primary question is "Why?" The causality of events is not nearly as crucial as the *meaning* of events. This is such a fundamental shift away from our presupposition of scientific naturalism that we can hardly *imagine* it. In other words, we first and automatically think of the event in terms of its metaphysical issues; its causes and its alignment with our conception of a closed universe governed by natural law. Then, and with some effort, we force ourselves to conceive of the universe as a place where divinity lay present in any moment, hidden behind the most ordinary things, ready to interject itself into our consciousness. We are not overwhelmed with wonder and awe. We are rather overwhelmed with *complexity*, the very notion intimating mechanical causality. How can we possibly expect to view the world as a living extension of a disguised divine reality when the question "Why?" barely penetrates our awareness?

---

[15] Halbertal and Margalit, *Idolatry*, p. 63.

The common *seneh*, a bush, nothing noteworthy, not even genus and species. Just any kind of insignificant bush becomes the vehicle of revelation of the greatest of mysteries, the divine name YHWH. It is, in fact, *unimaginable*. The God of glory, the

Creator, the Most High is manifest in the flame in a *bush*? That would be the equivalent of inviting the King of Jordan to a Presidential dinner and taking him to McDonalds. The insult would be beyond description. What jumps off the page for a Hebrew reader is not how God could be manifest in a material way but rather why the King of kings would ever allow such humiliation. If you don't know why, maybe you don't read the Scriptures like a Hebrew. Maybe the paradigm shift is much bigger than you thought.

24.

And YHWH Elohim said, "It is not good the man being alone. I will make for him an 'ezer kenegdo. Genesis 2:18

Order And Purpose

'ezer kenegdo – The opening of the Bible is a declaration of God's *ordering* the world. He is completely in control of all creation. His character is expressed in all that He does. His rule governs all He makes. Of course, this applies to human beings as well. What we notice is that God's ordered design always entails purpose. There are no accidents in this universe. Everything has a role to play, a purpose built into its design. In fact, this interdependency is so apparent throughout creation that even atheists find it difficult to explain. Order, design and purpose are so pervasive that no explanation of the world that ignores this fact can be considered valid. Accident does not produce ordered complexity.

This structural fact of existence allows us to ask a fundamental question about the *'ezer kenegdo*. If God makes everything for a purpose, what is the purpose of the *'ezer kenegdo*? The text clearly tells us that God *made* (implying with intentional purpose) the Woman. She was perfectly designed to fulfill *His* purpose. So if we want to know what that purpose is, we need to look at this text from God's point of view, not from the point of view of the beneficiary, Adam.

The text tells us that God was *motivated* to construct the *'ezer kenegdo* because of concern for the Man. But motivation is not purpose. Motivation explains why I make something, but that is not the same as what the creation does. God loved Adam. Adam was in need. His condition was not good in a universe designed around what is good. Therefore, something needed to be done. God produced the *'ezer kenegdo* in order to do something that would supply the need He observed.

In the past we explored in detail the connection between "good" and God's first instruction for living. Very briefly, God recognizes that Adam cannot fulfill the instruction without someone who is specifically designed to act as the guide, boundary-keeper and supporter of the instruction. The serpent attacks the *'ezer kenegdo* precisely because she is the guide, the boundary-keeper and the spiritual director. She determines the direction the first couple takes. Adam acknowledges his agreement with this purpose in his excuse for his behavior to God. The crucial point is this: *the 'ezer kenegdo is designed with a purpose in mind*. God made her that way. It is His ordering of the relationship between a husband and wife.

What does this mean today, after the collapse of Eden's delight and thousands of years of unordered living? It means that if we are going to restore the world to the righteousness God intended, we will have to reorder the relationship of marriage. We will have to recognize *and practice* the purpose of the *'ezer kenegdo*. We will have to realize that she was designed as the guide, the protector, the provider of spiritual awareness, the one who sets the boundaries for God's glory and our benefit. Whenever we refuse God's order, chaos follows. That is abundantly clear here, where the basic relationship of life is on the line. If you as a woman are not fulfilling your purpose as *'ezer kenegdo*, something is drastically wrong. You know it. You feel it. Now you need to do something about it. You were meant to be so close to God that your man sees God's hand in your life and knows that he is blessed in you. If you are a man, you need to let her be what she was meant to be, what she was designed to be and what you know she wants to be – for your benefit. Take off the shackles of control and follow your guide. Risk being blessed. What have you got to lose except your pride?

25.

*The **law of his God** is in his heart; his steps do not slip.* Psalm 37:31

Heaven On Earth

Law Of His God – David extols the righteous person. He describes God's delight in this person. He promises God's protection and blessing. He reminds the righteous of God's purposes fulfilled in their lives. He emphasizes the fact that the righteous do not slip or stumble. They know God's ways and confidently walk in them. Sounds pretty good, doesn't it? It even sounds good in English, but in Hebrew the full impact of David's review of the righteous explodes from the scroll. How is it that the righteous enjoy all these benefits? The answer is straightforward. The righteous know *torat Elohim*.

When we see the Hebrew words, we know David can have only one thing in mind. As far as David is concerned, the righteous live according to Torah, God's perfect instructions for a blessed life in this world and the world to come. If we had retained the Hebrew *torat* rather than translating the word with the English "law," we would have realized that David is not speaking about some inner principle of ethical action. He is not asking us to look into our hearts to find the sign of the Spirit or retreat to a private corner where we can concentrate on hearing God's voice. There is nothing private about David's view of God's ways. They are clearly revealed, written down for anyone to read. Torah is public, obvious and definitive. Just do what God says and your steps will not slip. No one reading the Hebrew text would have thought anything else.

But our English version shifts Torah to law. Yes, it can and does mean "law," but suddenly the tone of the word becomes ominous, threatening and limiting. Law means regulation, restriction and punishment. In our world, law carries the implication of forceful compliance where God becomes the universal moral policeman making sure we do everything exactly right – or else. Law reminds us of trials, sentences, prisons and men with guns. These are things the American consciousness bitterly rejects. In our world, *freedom* is the cry of the noble and courageous. No wonder so many otherwise devoted children of the Father squirm when someone like David suggests "law" is the way of the righteous.

I have always wondered why so many Christians believe the Law was done away with at the death of the Messiah. Actually, they believe that the Law was finished, completed and no longer applicable when "Jesus" dies on the cross. Now I realize that these wonderful people are probably reacting to a cultural extension of the word, not to the truth of God's way of living. They have been schooled so long in the Greek idea of freedom and in the American ideal of liberty that they cannot imagine a world where instructions in righteousness are the equivalent of laws of life. They have a pre-commitment to reading the text as *free people in a free society*, and so the very word strikes a discordant note of disdain. This is another tragedy of reading the Bible as if it were written for our society.

Every man and woman knows that life without a code of instructions is chaos and anarchy. We see daily examples of this lack of a code of behavior in the public schools and in government. No rule, no order. Since every Christian knows that God is a God of order, does it seem reasonable that He would have provided such orderly detail to Israel and then simply given the rest of us a general rule of thumb ("Love God and do as you please," or "WWJD")? That doesn't sound like a God who so carefully constructed the order of the universe that the butterfly effect is a reality. Would He leave His children in the dark, hoping they would find their own way among the weeds?

Torat Elohim is our slice of heaven on earth. It's the way the world really works - the first design. It's the goal of the restoration. Is there any reason not to put it into practice? Does our culture bias really count more than the words He revealed so long ago?

26.

*Hate evil, love good and establish justice in the **gate**; . . .*
Amos 5:15

Capitol Conditions

Gate – In the ancient near east, the city was protected by walls and a gate. The elders of the city sat in the gate, watching for strangers or circumstances that might be dangerous. As a result, political and social issues were settled where the elders sat – at the gate. The idiom "in the gate" (*vasha'ar*) means "where the politically and socially powerful conduct human affairs." The modern equivalent is the congress and the capitol. "In the gate" is wherever men (and women) determine the policies that govern the populace.

Amos' declaration poses immediate problems for our version of religion. In this Western culture, religion is a "personal" matter. From television pundits to famous preachers, we are taught that our experience with God is private. We believe in *personal* salvation, a relationship between the adherent and God Himself. We espouse the separation of Church and State. Amos' declaration falls outside the scope of religious consideration. Amos talks about *politics*, social policy and economic affairs, not about a heart-relationship with God. His suggestions are ruled illicit. In our world, preachers need to stay in the pulpit. Politicians sit in the gate.

Of course, it doesn't take very much reflection to evaluate what happens when men of God don't sit in the gate. Just look around. Is this what we really wanted? We have the "great society," but in every corner there is evil, rejection of the good and injustice. The nightly news is full of stories of corruption. The civilization practices immorality, idolatry and crimes against humanity without consequence. Who is responsible for this collapse? We are! We were supposed to be sitting in the gate. We were supposed to be guiding the community and the civilization from God's perspective. Amos doesn't say, "Now those who are believers should set up their own society." He says that we who are followers must enter into this society and take positions of power in order to bring God's order to the world. We are salt – the preservative of the moral order – and light – the beacon of justice. At least that is the intention. But we have opted for privacy. We have decided to abdicate the throne to those who seek it. We have retired from guidance and wisdom in order to protect our own castles. We have failed. We are guilty.

Now we face an enormous task. We must stand up and stand fast. We must take back the gate. Many will decry the effort claiming we have no right or authority. We have every right and all the authority. In fact, we have an *obligation* to sit in the gate because it is God's city. Cloistered environments and retired living are not God's objectives. We are here to redeem this world. The job won't be done until the gate belongs to the King.

If your life is circumscribed by your own castle walls, if you have barricaded yourself from the evil of the world, if you are afraid of the gate, then something is wrong. Amos calls you to change. Get up. Get out. Get going. Our faith is lived *in the world* where God is at work establishing justice.

27.

*You only have I known of all the families of the earth; **therefore** I will punish you for all your iniquities.* Amos 3:2

Elected To Suffer

Therefore – When will we finally forsake the populist idea that God saves us in order to make our lives prosperous? How foolish can we be? In a world that *hates* God, do we really imagine that His objective is to take us to the top of the world's pyramid? Behind such nonsense is nothing but selfish desire and arrogance. Amos gives us the real story, but it isn't a story that most "believers" either want to hear or are willing to embrace. The truth never hurt so much.

The Hebrew combination word *'al-ken* brings together a preposition and an adverb (adjective) to produce the idea of "thus by" or "thus for." This word connects the truth of the first statement with the truth of the second statement. Now read Amos 3:2 again. Did God choose one family of the earth as His to carry out His purpose to the nations? Yes, He did. Is that family the *only* family that is His exclusively and eternally? Yes, it is. What is the result of this election? If you expected Amos to recite all the blessings of Deuteronomy 28, you are in for a shock. The result of God's election is *punishment*. Why? Because His house is holy and His people are to be holy, and He will not restrain Himself from using whatever means is necessary to bring them to holiness. Without holiness they are unable to fulfill the mission of His election. Therefore, those whom He has called can expect to *suffer* not only because they oppose the idolatry of the world but also because God is stripping them of their own internal idolatry in order to make them pure instruments in His hand.

Do you want to get off the train now? Every follower of YHWH is called to stand against the world. This means living according to principles that will *inevitably* bring conflict with the idolatrous culture that surrounds us. We should not be surprised. We should be exuberant because this conflict demonstrates that we are fulfilling His purposes. At the same time, God promises to shape us, and quite often that process is painful. Quite often it feels like punishment. But it is not *wrath*. Punishment has purpose. It is designed to bring conformity to purity. Once more, when we are punished, it is a sign of God's election. The man who does not know God feels no pain over his sin. God's punishment is the assurance that He cares enough to correct us. It is the assurance that we have been chosen for His plan. It is the sign of His love.

Don't get off the train! Look beyond the immediate. Don't fall prey to the idolatry of the culture, an idolatry that concentrates on gratification rather than transformation. Allow God's hand to reprove and correct, knowing that He never punishes without purpose and that His purposes are always to bring His chosen into alignment with the design of the perfect creation. God's anvil makes only one kind of weapon – a perfect one.

28.

*Then Yeshua said to His disciples, "If any one wishes to come after Me, let him **deny** himself, and take up his cross, and follow me."* Matthew 16:24

Spiritual Gains

Deny – What does Yeshua's statement mean to you? Do you think of denial in terms of turning away from pointless affluence, seductive pleasures or immoral behavior? Do you think that Yeshua intended us to refuse our own selfish desires in order to submit to God's higher purposes? Perhaps we gain a deeper understanding of the nature of denial when we apply this instruction to the specific arena of money. Jacques Ellul helps us see this connection when he says, "When God attacks this power [money] that has us in its grip because it has aroused our love, when he tears away a treasure to which we have become attached, he is attacking us. God's deliverance is not a stroke of a magic wand which leaves us intact, the way we were. It is a rescue of part of ourselves. Consequently we may have the impression, the feeling, of being amputated, diminished. God who is delivering us from the shackles of this power, is also destroying its roots which have taken hold of us."[16] In other words, the act of denial is an invitation to let God amputate. It isn't simply refusing to do something we really want to do. It is asking God to *cut it out of our hearts.*

The Greek verb *aparneomai* means "to renounce, to disown." Yeshua reminds us that renouncing other lovers is a *requirement* of following Him. This is no different than the requirement of the first commandment. YHWH has exclusive right to the love of His children and He will tolerate *no* rival, even if that rival has roots deep within our own personalities. Exorcism must follow. The fact that Yeshua demands such exclusivity in a Jewish culture is another indication that He is God manifest in the flesh. If this were not the case, His requirement could be nothing but idolatry.

Consider what this means for our world's preoccupation with money. Money and wealth are not the same. Money is a *tool*. It is to be used as a tool. That means it has no intrinsic value. It is not something to be enjoyed in itself. It is to be used to bring about those purposes and plans that enrich life and advance the Kingdom. God grants wealth. He grants it to those who are equipped to accomplish His purposes with their abundance. Not all respond appropriately to His gift. The consequences of this rejection will be worked out in the Judgment. Not all are wealthy, but money touches everyone. Whenever we convert money into a goal rather than a tool, we invest value into it and make it into an idol. God intends us to *use* money, not to *collect* it. In fact, money has no purpose aside from its use to bring about restoration. That doesn't mean it is only used for

---

[16] Jacques Ellul, *Money and Power*, p. 85.

evangelism. That is too limited. Money is a tool that should be used to enhance life. It is life that has value. Money is simply a means to bring life to the full.

Does that mean our objective is to have as much comfort and convenience as money can buy? Of course not. Wherever life suffers from lack of money, we who have the *tool* need to apply it. Believe me, there are enormous opportunities to enhance life that do not include jet skis and iPods. When those opportunities are fulfilled, then there will be time to think about jet skis.

Let's consider one simple example. The norms of business often provide commission payments in financial deals. Good business could be defined as doing everything according to the norms – or – we could act on the basis of Kingdom ethics, deny that money is anything more than a tool, and be *generous* toward others whenever we are able. We can remove the power of money by refusing to allow it to determine our behavior.

Is God amputating a bit of your worldview today? Are you assisting Him in the exorcism of subtle idolatry?

29.

*The earth is also **polluted** by its inhabitants, for they transgressed laws, violated statutes, broke the everlasting covenant. Therefore, a curse devours the earth, and those who live in it are held guilty.* . Isaiah 24:5-6

Economic Advice

Polluted – It's the economy, stupid! Everyone is concerned. Everyone is worried (almost everyone). But no one seems to know what to do. Change, change, change. We might as well throw money to the wind. Until we listen to YHWH's economic advice (and do what it says), all the changes won't really matter. It's His earth. It's His order. Working against the grain of the universe won't fix anything.

Isaiah delivered pertinent economic advice thousands of years ago. The world won't produce because its inhabitants have polluted it. Of course, Isaiah is *not* talking about oil spills and garbage dumps. The Hebrew word is _haneph_. It means defiled, corrupted, profaned. The world is polluted by moral decay, not environmental disaster. Human sin has a direct bearing on the earth itself. The land is polluted by disobedience, and no amount of effort will stop the pollution until obedience to the Creator becomes the norm. If we want economic prosperity, we can dispense with the committees and the regulators and the bureaucrats. We can replace all the entitlements and the stimulus packages and the bailouts. What we need is repentance. We are Nineveh. Our forty days are about to end. Until sackcloth and ashes are the latest fashion, there will be no brake on the decline. The economy is *not* the problem. *We are the problem!*

Haneph is associated with specific actions. These include the shedding of blood, divorce, breaking covenant obligations, corrupt priests and officials, association with deceivers, lack of active compassion for the oppressed, wealth that ignores the homeless, the widows and the orphans, and reliance on pacts with other nations. History demonstrates what God guarantees. No civilization has ever survived moral pollution of the land. Have we forgotten that the earth is the Lord's?

Buber says, " the human lot is decided by the dialogue between God and man, the reality of which fill the whole life and the whole world,.." [17] He notes that the separation of

---

[17] Martin Buber, *The Prophetic Faith*, p. 90.

religion from the operations of the state "claims to take from God's actual leadership and from man's actual response their character of reality, by fostering the mythico-cultic sphere independently of individual and public ways of life."[18] In other words, when we remove God as King and replace Him with the governance of men, we construct a government of idolatry and *it will not stand*. The most important function of governance is the obligation of officials to demonstrate obedience to YHWH and to insure the people follow His ways. No other social arrangement will survive. Jonah has arrived in spite of his resistance. The call has sounded forth.

30.

*they desire to **draw near** to God* Isaiah 58:2

The Second Idolatry

Draw Near – Yesterday we learned that *qirbah* is used only twice in Scripture. This is the second occurrence: *qirvat Elohiym*. Asaph desired only that God should be near. Now Isaiah tells the people that their pleas for God's presence are in vain. Why? Because they refuse to accept the pictograph of *qareb*. They want God to be close, but that don't want to humble themselves. Read Isaiah's accusation. "Look! Your fasts are motivated by strife and contention. You want to strike with a wicked fist. You are arrogant in your religious rituals. Do you think that is what I want?" God goes on. "You think bowing your head and putting on sackcloth shows your humility, but I see nothing but pride. Let me tell you what kind of fast I want. Remove wickedness!

Let the oppressed go free! Divide your bread with the

---

[18] Martin Buber, *The Prophetic Faith*, p. 85.

hungry and your clothes with the naked. Do not hide yourself from your own sin!" Ouch!

Do you want to draw near to God? Do you want Him to draw near to you? Asaph knew that being in His presence was the only good thing in life. That is *all* Asaph wanted. Isaiah reminds us that drawing near is not a function of religious ritual. It is a matter of social justice! And God's version of social justice (the only version that counts) begins with *humility*! Get rid of the wickedness you harbor in your life and your community. Expel the corruption. Vomit the violence. Cast away the unrighteousness. Then act with benevolence toward the oppressed, the hungry and the homeless. *Share* yourself and your on-loan assets! Divide what you have among those in need. Lend a hand to help them up. Show them mercy and kindness. Don't hide behind your self-righteous status. Be vulnerable. You were once a slave in Egypt too.

No man draws near to God on a golden chariot. And God approaches no man who is not willing to bow down before the King. We have to spend some time feeding pigs before we can realize the honor that comes with being a servant in His house.

Qirbah may only be used twice in Scripture, but those two occasions are very instructive. One shows us the intensity of a man who desires God at any cost. The other shows us the wayward delusion of a people who think they have earned a right to demand that God draw near. It is a sad fact that most people are described by the second occurrence of *qirbah* rather than the first.

What have we learned? From Asaph we learn that "it is not important what dying appears to be in the eyes of man: if he lives in communion with God, he knows that God is eternal and that He is his 'portion'."[19] From Isaiah we learn that the practice of religion is a sham if it is devoid of humility within community. Ritual means nothing if it is not accompanied by justice. We learn that we can, in fact, command God's presence – by being His hands and feet to those in need. What is my good? To be with God. And where is He? With those who need Him most.

Where are you?

31.

*You are the **anointed cherub** that covers, I have set you so*
Ezekiel 28:14

Adam's Real Sin

Anointed Cherub – Ezekiel's prophetic announcement to the king of Tyre describes more than we might think. Ezekiel provides us with a midrash on Adam. We need to pay close attention to the prophet's words since they tell us a great deal about God's intention for creating human beings. "You were in Eden, the garden of God," Ezekiel writes. This is certainly not historically true of the king of Tyre, but it is true if we look at the general pattern of human behavior as seen in our progenitor, Adam. The prophet tells us that Adam had it all. Everything was prepared for him. He was placed on the holy mountain of God, blameless from the moment of his creation. He was anointed cherub.

Now what does that mean? What do the cherubs do? The word *kerub* isn't used very often in Scripture. Our English word *cherubim* is a transliteration of the Hebrew *kerubim*

---

[19] Martin Buber, *The Prophetic Faith*, p. 201.

(plural), not a translation. Why? The root word *kerub* is supposed to be the past participle of the verb *karab* (according to the way Hebrew nouns are formed), but this verb does not exist in Hebrew. The word does occur as a noun in other places, some of which are quite interesting: Genesis 3:24, Psalm 99:1 and Psalm 18:10. The design of the cherubim above the ark is similar to the

description found in the vision of Ezekiel (1:4-14). Ezekiel adds to the picture in 10:18-22. You can compare this with John's vision in Revelation 4:6-8. The *kerubim* were assigned the task of keeping sinful Adam and Havvah out of the Garden. Their images also guarded the ark of the covenant, standing on both sides of the mercy seat covering. In other words, they are guardians of God's purposes for righteousness. Now Ezekiel tells us that *Adam* was supposed to play that role. He was anointed to guard (cover) the Garden, the representation of God's good creation.

But something happened.

Ezekiel's prophetic word describes the tragic event of Adam's sin as *idolatry*. Adam served the serpent rather than YHWH. Adam listened to the voice of the serpent rather than the voice of YHWH. Adam *remembered* the words of the serpent but forgot the words of YHWH. Adam, not Eve, made the deliberate choice to serve himself and someone other than YHWH. Adam was created for leadership (*mashah* – anointed – is often used to describe a ceremonial ritual designating a leader). What kind of leadership? The leadership of the *kerub*, the guardian of God's Garden, the protector of all that is good in the eyes of the Lord. But Adam took care of himself. He became the guardian of his own interests. That made him an idolater and required God to remove him from the Garden of Good. By the way, Havvah was also appointed a guardian – the guardian of Adam.

Men, do we want to recover the role YHWH gave us when we were created His image bearers? Then guard what He says is good. Guard His righteousness. Guard His name. Protect His creation against the sedition of the enemy. Become the anointed *kerubim* that He made us to be. The objective is crystal clear.

God leaves no doubt about what He says is good. Our job is to *protect* His order of creation. In doing so, we will ensure the well being of every worshipper. A little less than angels? You bet! And for very good reasons. Will you take up the angelic role God assigned?

Oh yes, this anointed role is not accomplished alone. Women have a covenant relationship with the Lord to protect their men and bring blessings into their lives by making sure we men protect God's good. It's a big job, especially since men have a propensity to act like Adam.

32.

*"Behold, to obey **is better than** sacrifice, and to listen better than the fat of rams."* 1 Samuel 15:22

The Man Who Would Be King

Is Better Than – Saul loved being king. He loved to be the man in charge. He loved to make the decisions. That love of power and prestige ruined him. He forgot that the king is called to have an ear for the words of the Lord. He forgot that the only reason a man leads is because he first serves. Saul thought he could pacify YHWH with ritual, but Samuel reminded him that ritual means nothing if it is used to replace obedience. The Hebrew preposition *min* has a half dozen or more meanings depending on the context. Here it is used as the indicator of comparison. It could be translated "to obey is above sacrifice," or " to obey is beyond sacrifice," or "to obey is greater than sacrifice." What is really important is the implication that failing to carry out God's commands is the equivalent of rebellion, iniquity and idolatry (see the next verse). Samuel speaks ominous words to Saul: "Because you have rejected the word of YHWH, YHWH has also rejected you from being king." Disobedience has terrible consequences because disobedience is tantamount to serving some other god.

Many know this story but few consider its contemporary application. Who are the people who substitute ritual for obedience? It isn't the non-believers. They don't care about the ritual at all. Only those who are connected to the worship of YHWH are likely to use ritual as an alternative to obedience. We are those people.

"How can you say that?" you might ask. "We worship God. We believe in Jesus. We go to church." So? The issue is not about religious practice or sacred rituals. It's about doing what YHWH says. As far as I can tell, YHWH says to watch what you eat, use your assets according to His instructions, demonstrate justice and righteousness over excess gain, sacrifice for others, love enemies, honor elders and respect His creation. In fact, He gives specific commandments about exactly how to accomplish these things, including how to worship Him. But it seems that a large number of Christian practices follow Saul. They substitute what God said for some ritual, perhaps a ritual that even has a biblical connection. But there's just a little alteration, a little twist, a little difference. And when YHWH rejects those substitutions as idolatry, we get upset, claiming that we have the right *motivation*. Really? What motivates us to make up our own rules for obedience? G. K. Beale makes a comment about Israel's history that seems particularly appropriate for us. "The problem with these traditions was not that they were necessarily unbiblical or bad in and of themselves, but Israel's attitude to the traditions. Israel trusted in these traditions instead of in God and his word."[20] What do you suppose Yeshua meant when He said, "Neglecting the commandments of God, you hold fast to the traditions of men" (Mark 7:8)?

John Stott said, "The hallmark of an authentic evangelicalism is not the uncritical repetition of old traditions but the willingness to submit every tradition, however ancient, to fresh biblical scrutiny and, if necessary, reform." Do you think he's right? Have you reconsidered the "traditions" of your faith and asked if they match the words of YHWH? Have you taken a long, hard look at the actual words of YHWH, or does your faith rest on the traditions of your church? Is it really better to obey or will that just cause too much conflict in your life?

33.

*For God knows that in the day you eat of it, then your eyes shall be opened, and you shall be as gods, **knowing** good and evil.* Genesis 3:5 (my translation)

Opening The Door

Knowing – Adam opened the door. That's the way Paul puts it in his letter to the Roman congregation. "As by one man sin entered" uses a Greek verb that suggests opening a door. Adam let sin in. You might ask why Paul doesn't say that Eve opened the door, but that question belongs to another day. Today we will look at what is implied in the serpent's suggestion. How does eating this fruit make it possible to know good and evil? Once again, it's all about a door.

---

[20] G. K. Beale, *We Become What We Worship*, p. 169.

"God knows," says the serpent. "The problem in your life, woman, is that you don't know in the same way God knows. Oh, you know what God says. I can see that. You can quote His words. But all you're doing is mimicking Him. You don't really *know* what it means to decide between good and evil. You're a bit *deficient* in that area. But you *could* know if you just decide to take things into your own hands."

The verse uses the Hebrew verb *yada* in both occurrences of "know." *Yada* is a very big verb. *Yada* covers everything from knowing that 2+2=4 to knowing the intimacy of sexual relations. In this verse, the power of *yada* is revealed in its pictograph. Yod-Daleth-Ayin paints the picture "to make the door of experience." In other words, *yada* is about making something happen. What will I make happen? I will make a way to open the door of experience for myself. I will walk my path through the door into the world where I have experiential knowledge, where I have participated in the matter at hand. Why is Ḥavvah tempted to eat from the Tree? Because she believes that eating of the Tree will *improve* her ability to make decisions on her own. She won't have to rely on the manual anymore. Now she will *intuitively* know what to do. She will have *experience*.

Isn't this a common temptation among us today? Don't we still desire to "just get a taste of it" so we can decide for ourselves rather than relying on the word of someone else? The appeal of the Tree is the suggestion that I can cut my own path. The promise of the Tree is that I will no longer be *dependent* on another. The sin of Adam and Ḥavvah is *idolatry*. "Disguised polytheism is also the religion of him who combines with the worship of God the devotion to his *own* gain."[21]

---

[21] Abraham Heschel, *God In Search Of Man*, p. 392

"God, I worship You. I know You want me to be all that I can be. So, just help me be a little more prosperous, a little more independent, a little more self-reliant. Just make me more capable of taking care of myself. Just help me accomplish my goals in life. Then I'll even worship You better." Making our own way is eating from the Tree. But now you *know* better, don't you?

34.

*Now the Bereans were of more noble character than the Thessalonians, for they received the message with great eagerness and examined the Scriptures every day **to see if** what Paul said was true.* Acts 17:11 (NIV)

To Be Berean

To See If – Are you Berean? Are you willing to examine the Scriptures every day to see if what you are being taught is true? Ah, there are some implicit assumptions here that must be acknowledged. First, the "Scriptures" are the words of God found in the Tanakh – the Older Testament. Believe me when I tell you that the Bereans were not reading commentaries on Romans or the gospel of John. They determined the truth of Paul's claims based entirely on the material from Genesis to Malachi. Do you do that?

Second, the standard for their authority was the Tanakh. They searched the Scriptures, the Hebrew Scriptures, to determine if Paul's message aligned with the revealed word of God. They didn't run to the pastor for his view or look up the creed or the doctrine of the church or grab Geisler's systematic theology. They went to the text – the Jewish, Hebrew authoritative text for their lives – to see if what Paul was teaching found its source in their holy code. How about you? When you hear a sermon or read a new religious book *or listen to the news or read a newspaper*, are you running to the Tanakh to see if what you are hearing is in line with God's truth? Do you live by His book? Does what you hear match His words? If Paul's message to the Bereans didn't square with Scripture, then it was garbage, deception and a lie. Are you careful enough to check what you believe with the instructions from God?

Third, the Bereans received Paul's message with great eagerness. They did not take a skeptical stance. They were committed to learning, to examining, to discussing, to growing in their understanding of God's word. If Paul brought something new, great! Let's listen! Let's hear him. Then we will go to work checking it out. What about you? Are you ready, anticipating challenge, anxious to know, eager to explore? Does the careful examination of God's word *thrill* you?

And finally, the Bereans rushed to the Scriptures every day in order *to see if* (in Greek, *ei echoi tauta outos* – literally "if have these so") these things were true. "If" (*ei*) is one of the most important words in the Bible. "If" means that the truth of the claim is conditional. *You need to look at the evidence.* There are no "face-value" claims in this faith. God demonstrates His trustworthiness with real evidence. But you have to go look at it. He isn't doing to show up with a neon sign or a billboard in the sky or a slap across the face. *You* have to do some work. *You* have to examine, search, press, think and compare. You have to become a Berean.

We might come to the faith because it is part of our culture or our upbringing, but that isn't enough to make it deep and real. Rush to examine. That's the key. Go see *if* it's true. Today!

35.

*I YHWH and none else, forming light and creating darkness; making peace and **creating** evil – I YHWH do all these things.* Isaiah 45:6-7 (translation: Martin Buber)

The Problem Of Evil

Creating – Where did evil come from? Such a simple question. Such an enormously difficult answer, if there even is an answer. One of the greatest impediments to belief in a wholly good God is the existence of evil. For centuries theologians have struggled to find a resolution to the problem. How can a good God be the *final* creator of all things and yet there be evil in the universe? Usually we try to make a very big dent with an explanation about free choice and sin. But some things just don't seem to be explained by these facts. Some things just seem too hideous to be accounted for by human failure. When pressed *really hard*, theologians turn to this passage in Isaiah, claiming that even though we can't understand *how* this can be true, the Bible clearly states that God is not in competition with some other equally powerful demonic force. Evil does not have *independent* existence.

But maybe the appeal to Isaiah isn't quite right. Maybe Isaiah's cultural setting has more to say about this statement than the hoped-for resolution of the theological problem of evil. Martin Buber thinks so.

Buber suggests that Isaiah's statement must be understood in the context of the 4th Century BC. In that culture, Babylonian astral gods were the creators of light and darkness and the progenitors of the second-order divine beings who caused good and evil to exist. These astral gods belonged to a tribal hierarchy of divine entities, ruling over the fate of men and requiring appeasement before showing favor. Isaiah destroys this pagan belief by claiming that "YHVH is absolutely different, as He reveals Himself to Cyrus in the word of the prophet. He creates by Himself not only the cosmic opposition pair light-darkness, but also that which constitutes the human sphere, peace-evil. That *shalom*, "peace," "welfare," and not *tov*, "good," is here contrasted with *ra*, "evil," is obviously in order to keep away the notions of ethical opposition. Evil in the sense of wickedness comes into the world only as a result of resistance to God; but evil in the sense of adversity and affliction . . . is fashioned by God Himself for purposes of His leadership of the world, without gaining thereby the same standing as peace, since in the last resort this rules alone."[22]

It's worth noting that the verb for "create" in this statement is *bara'*, a verb used exclusively with God as the subject (cf. Genesis 1:1 and Isaiah 65:17). Here it is applied *only* to the negatives "darkness" and "evil." "Light" and "peace" use the verbs *yatsar* and *asah*. The emphasis is theological. No pagan god or gods bring about any conditions of opposition in the cosmos or in the human realm. God is God *alone*! He is the *only* divine creator.

In the end, Isaiah's statement does not answer the question: Where did evil come from? It stands as a declaration of sovereignty in a cultural of pagan polytheism. It's focus is on the immediate need to overthrow idolatry. Isaiah's statement cannot be lifted from its cultural setting and forced into a box within the plan of the systematic theologian. In the end, we discover that God is *in history*, interacting with the needs of the day, involving Himself in the issues at hand. The Holy One of Israel is not the God of the eternal "present," far above the petty concerns of human

---

[22] Martin Buber, *The Prophetic Faith*, p. 213.

beings. God creates in history; a history that is found in the realm of men, filled with the issues of men. If we want to meet God, we will have to dress for the occasion in the garb of the day of His revelation.

36.

*Surely our griefs He Himself **bore**, and our sorrows He carried; yet we ourselves esteemed Him stricken, smitten of God and afflicted.* Isaiah 53:4

How To Read Isaiah

Bore – We love to read Isaiah as if it were written for us, that is, for Christians who believe "Jesus" is the Son of God who came to forgive people of their sins. At the Christmas season, we read Isaiah as Christian prophecy. Of course, it is perfectly valid to do so, but it's hard to imagine that Isaiah's audience would have understood the text in this way. After all, our exegesis depends entirely on hindsight, and hindsight is usually pretty accurate. What would happen to these verses if we asked, "How would the people of Isaiah's time understand what he said?"

We don't have to delve into ancient history to find some clues. All we have to do is read Jewish scholars. Since they don't accept Yeshua as the Jewish Messiah, they must have another way of explaining these verses. When we look, we discover some useful insights; insights that enlarge our own Christian prophetic views of the text.

"These iniquities, which he has borne, are not those of Israel, concerning which it was publicly announced that they were already atoned for by their affliction."[23] Isaiah writes that Israel's atonement occurs through its suffering. In fact,

---

[23] Martin Buber, *The Prophetic Faith*, p. 227.

Israel has paid twice over for its sin. Perhaps we are a bit too quick to think that *all* sin is atoned for by the sacrifice of Yeshua. Doesn't God Himself say that Israel's suffering and affliction has paid the required price? Buber continues, "It was already known since the prophecy of Amos . . . that among all the peoples, Israel are the people which God Himself visits for their offenses, and when they return in repentance He Himself redeems them; no one can interfere in this matter. The people receive correction from God's own hand; but again it is God Himself Who 'bears' Israel's offenses." Then Buber adds a small explanatory note: "this verb must not be weakened to mean forgiveness only."[24]

Buber's Jewish view is very different than the usual Christian view because Buber gives full weight to the exclusive election of Israel. The question of salvation is not aimed at Israel. Israel knows how it is saved. It is saved through the suffering it experiences at the hand of the Lord. The question is how will the sinful nations be saved? How will the *rest of the world* come to the Lord? If God Himself bears the sin of Israel (and not simply "forgives" them), then what will happen with all those who are *not* Israel? This is the question confronting the suffering servant of YHWH. In other words, the context of Isaiah's prophecy is the *idolatry* of the 5th Century BC in which the nations turned to false gods for redemption. Isaiah reveals that these false gods are powerless to save. It is Israel's God who saves. He has demonstrated His willingness to bear the iniquities of Israel and He is sending His servant to do the same for the nations. In Buber's view, the servant is both a personal and Israel, wrapped up together in this motif of suffering for another. We may disagree from the perspective of hindsight about the *person* of the Messiah, but we should not miss the point

---

[24] Buber, p. 227.

Buber makes regarding the role of suffering in redemption. The Hebrew verb *nasa'* means "to carry, to lift away, to bear." Buber draws our attention to the fact that this verb implies direct, personal involvement, not simply forensic (legal) dismissal. God does not so easily forgive that it requires nothing more than a change in the entry of the ledger. God *bears* the actual iniquities. They are piled upon Him. He *suffers* under their load. This theme is revolutionary, radical and irresistible. There is no other god who takes the sin of the people upon himself. Only YHWH, the one true God. And there is no other faith that could imagine God would Himself willingly accept such a burden. The suffering of Israel as a means of atonement is but an example of the suffering of Israel's God atoning for the sins of the nations.

Perhaps what is happening in the death and resurrection of our Messiah is a great deal more than simple forgiveness. Perhaps we learn something about who God is when we examine the text with Jewish eyes.

Excursus:
Erga tes Sarkos (Works of the Flesh)

Galatians 5:19-21

Part of understanding the biblical view of idolatry is an appreciation for the behaviors that result from idolatry. Sha'ul gives us an expanded catalog of these behaviors in the letter to the Galatians. By examining the vocabulary of this passage, we will have a more robust view of what idolatry looks like in action.

Christians have always been taught to avoid sin. That's a given. But sometimes I think we trip ourselves up by not really understanding what the Bible calls "sin". We assume that we know what we aren't supposed to do. Murder, steal, lie, covet (that one is kind of vague but it's on the list), use God's name in vain – we could add a few more from memory. Unfortunately, we tend to generalize sins with a "don't hurt anyone" morality. We don't spend much time actually understanding the details of what we are fighting. Since we usually don't commit those "big" ones (murder, stealing, adultery, lying – well, maybe not lying), we don't give much thought to the rest of the list.

There are several very specific lists of sins in the Bible. These are detailed descriptions of the actions that God wants us to avoid at all costs. Paul gives us one of these lists in his letter to the Galatians:

> adultery, fornication, uncleanness, lasciviousness, idolatry, witchcraft, hatred, variance, emulations, wrath, strife, seditions, heresies, envyings, murders, drunkenness, revellings and such like

These actions are so serious that he goes on to give us a dire warning. If you practice these things, you will not inherit the kingdom of God. Could the warning be any stronger? I don't think so. Paul is saying that if you repeatedly perform (the word is *prassontes* – it means "to do over and over") these actions, you and God will part company.

These are high stakes. Wouldn't it make sense to know exactly what Paul's list means? Would you ever go into a life and death battle without doing some "intel" on the enemy's behavior? I don't think so. Yet many Christians seem oblivious of the true scope and depth of any of these actions. It's about time we learned something more about the "works of the flesh".

Before we look at the description of each of these actions, we need to notice some patterns. Four of the seventeen actions are about sex. Two are about sorcery. Six are about anger. Only one is about beliefs. Two are about inappropriate intoxicated behavior. Only four have obvious connections to the Ten Commandments. On this basis alone, problems with anger and sex outweigh all other concerns. Of course, Paul is not suggesting a ranked-order of sins, some less important than others. He clearly says that the practice of *any* of these will break fellowship with God. But it is interesting that the ones he lists most often are inter-personal sins. They are sins about how we act toward each other. Apparently God thinks that behavior between human beings is pretty important.

Let's take a look at the details to see what's on Paul's mind.

Adultery – the word Paul uses is *moicheia*. This word does not appear in most modern translations. That's because the current best scholarly edition of the Greek text from the oldest manuscripts does not have the word *moicheia* in it. That word is found in the Textus Receptus, the Greek text available when the King James Bible was translated. So, if you compare the King James to modern translations, you will see this difference.

But even if it was added to the text later, it has quite an important history. It is the same word Jesus uses when he speaks of the evil that proceeds from a man's heart. In the Greek translation of the Old Testament, it is the word found in Jeremiah and Hosea when the prophets tell the people of God that they have whored after other gods. It is a very strong and fairly clear word. It means exactly what we think it means – illicit sex with someone who is married to another. However, the range of this word is a little bigger than the act of intercourse. It also means "to seduce" or "to be seduced" and it carries the sense of using deception and cunning to get control of someone. Here the word describes one of the actions of a larger class of actions called *porneias*. This larger group of actions is the next word in our list.

In order to understand why Jesus and Paul include adultery in the list of sins that separate us from God, we have to know a bit more about the contemporary culture of the first Century. The Greeks viewed adultery as a one-sided affair (pun intended). The prohibition against illicit sex with a married person applied basically only to women. Men were more or less expected to have sex with other single women and these actions were commonplace in the Greek and Roman world. In fact, the proliferation of sexual relations outside marriage became so great that one of the Roman Emperors actually passed a law against it – a law that had almost no effect on curbing the practice.

The Old Testament has a lot to say about adultery. God's

commandment against adultery establishes the commitment of partners in marriage as one of the most important foundations of community life. When confronted by the Pharisees on the issue of divorce, Jesus refers to God's intention in marriage, not to the actual practices of men. The reason for demanding fidelity in marriage is not only protection of the family. Marital fidelity is also a symbolic representation of exclusive loyalty to God. How we respect our vows with another person is a reflection of how we respect our commitments to God. This is the reason that prophets use the symbols of fidelity and adultery to point out the apostasy of Israel.

But even in the Old Testament, the focus of adultery is on the adulterous *woman*. Obligation for fidelity rests on her. However, when Jesus and Paul used this word, they made it clear that the proper context involved both male and female partners in a marriage. For the first time in thousands of years, women were granted the same responsibility and the same *respect* as men. Neither party had license to pursue sexual relations with another person. God's ideal of monogamous commitment was re-instated. In addition, Jesus amplified the requirement by teaching that the lustful desire for another was equivalent to the act of sexual exploitation. Adultery was not confined to the physical sexual act. It was a matter of the heart. In a culture that regarded sexual relations as commonplace as any other physical pleasure, this requirement radically separated early Christian believers from their contemporaries. Women were to be no less respected than men when it came to the unconditional divine command to love as Christ has loved. Women were not property and were not to be treated as such. Men were called to exhibit the same exclusive loyalty to their spouses that they would show to their God. The consequences for violating God's intention were clear:

> Marriage is to be held in honor among all, and the marriage bed is to be undefiled; for fornicators and adulterers God will judge (Heb. 13:4)

Now that adultery is no longer the special burden of women alone, believers are told quite clearly that engaging in the attempt to seduce, being seduced, considering and contemplating seduction and, of course, completing the act of seduction is a direct affront to the God who created us male and female. It circumvents His sovereignty by proclaiming (usually in secret) that I have the right to do what I wish with my body. That, says Paul, is entirely wrong. God gave you your body. It is His right to tell you how you are to treat it.

King David seduced Bathsheba. He violated God's sacred intention. When he was confronted and he repented, he did not go first to Bathsheba to ask forgiveness. He went to God. He knew that his sin was in God's face. Adultery is about our desire to dictate to God how we will use our bodies. That is a "right" we do not have.

The next word is **fornication** - *porneias*. We already know this word. It is the root word of pornography (*graphe* means "writing"). It comes from a word that means "to sell". In the Greek world, slaves were often the targets of sexual abuse. This word describes selling slaves who were used for sex, in other words, prostitutes. The word was expanded to cover all sorts of sexual abuse including intercourse with either female or male prostitutes, sexual favors with or without actual intercourse and homosexuality. A great deal of this activity was conducted under religious sanctions. The temple of Aphrodite had more than 1000 temple prostitutes. Surprisingly, brothels were not known in ancient Greece. This is because there was no prohibition against masters using their slaves for sexual encounters.

Later, a change in Greek law that denied foreigners civil rights forced many women to make money through sex. But the biggest issue contributing to prostitution and sexual promiscuity in Greece was the Greek view of life. Sex outside marriage was considered as natural as eating and drinking. Only excesses were censured. No moral stigma was placed on usual sexual behavior.

This cultural view was the completely opposite of the Hebrew idea of sexual activity. Prostitution existed in the Hebrew culture but sexual involvement with prostitutes was strictly condemned. The basis of sexual behavior was found in the idea of a pure and holy God. Sexual activity was a reflection of the divine activity of creation and as such was under the direct command of God. The Hebrew nation was surrounded by cultures that practiced religious prostitution in fertility cults. Many fertility cults believed that having sex within the religious community would insure prosperous crops. God's law made strict provisions for separating the Hebrew people from these practices. God Himself was the provider of prosperity. No action of man, sexual or otherwise, was allowed to diminish the acknowledgement of God's rule over the earth.

In addition, God used marriage as a symbol of His choosing a people of His own, just as a husband chose a bride. The choice belonged to God, not to the people. Their conduct was supposed to reflect the same faithfulness and loyalty prescribed for marriage. Marriage was raised from a merely social institution to a sacred portrayal of God's election.

In the first Century, the Greek and Hebrew cultural differences were in constant tension. But the New Testament concedes nothing to the Greek view. Jesus strengthened the view of the Old Testament by condemning all sexual activity outside of marriage, even if it was only in thoughts. Paul reinforced this view in his battle against the predominant cultural values of the Roman Empire. God's people are called apart from the values of the world. They are to practice holiness in every part of their lives. Obviously, no activity is more important in this regard than sex. The Old Testament foundation of God's election and God's sovereignty still stands as the reason for sexual purity, but the concept is now given explicit connection to the entire believing community. No sexual impurity or vice has any part in the body of believers and if tolerated, brings guilt and condemnation on the whole group. Paul ties sexual impurity to a lack of a pure heart (unclean) and on that basis is able to say that no one who practices such acts will be part of God's kingdom. In Revelation, John uses the word *proneuo* as a summary description of all of the sins encompassed by those who oppose God's rule.

Today we live in a culture of pluralism and accommodation. Gay rights, sexual freedom and adult lifestyles permeate every part of our world. Our contemporary culture is not significantly different from the non-believing culture of the first Century. I recently read a best-selling novel. In the book, the male hero had sexual encounters with several women, some married and some not. At one point, the author put these words into the mouth of the hero: "Sex is what adults do when they date". Unfortunately, today we need to re-write that line to remove the word "adult". Sex is the by-word of the culture (we will have more to learn about this with the next word). Ethnic groups in our culture pride themselves on male conquest, but the truth is that every male is subject to the temptation of adultery. Today we may have medical or social reasons to abstain, but none of these are sufficient to resolve the issue from God's perspective. Sex is about life and God says life is sacred. Therefore, sex reflects a sacred relationship, a divine encounter blessed by the Creator. Anything that treats it otherwise is suspect.

Some religious groups have tried to argue that homosexuality is prohibited only for those who act against their nature, that is, they are really heterosexuals but are engaging in homosexual acts. The intention behind this argument is to further the claim that those people who are "born" homosexual or for whom homosexual behavior is "natural" are not under God's judgment since they are behaving the way God made them. There is a word for this kind of argument in Greek – a word that they seem to ignore. It is *moros* and it means "without moral character". The argument is purely an attempt to justify what God clearly condemns. I'm sorry, but God doesn't care why or how you got involved in homosexuality. He only cares that you repent and stop. Does that seem harsh? So is God's wrath. Of course, God does care about the homosexual. He knows the struggles and defeats, the trauma and discouragement. But the fact remains that this behavior is sinful. And God promises that no temptation is too much for us to endure when we turn our lives completely over to His purposes.

Pornography, sexual promiscuity, titillation, seduction, homosexuality, indifferent attitudes toward sex, immodest behavior, careless disregard and uncontrolled actions are *porneias*. The culture is immersed in all of this. From billboards to movies, from radio shows to novels, we are afloat on a sea of *porneias*. Most of us react against the gross indulgences. But most of us allow the "minor" infractions. We are so saturated that we begin to become immune to God's claims of purity. The reason is quite obvious. Sex is one of the most powerful influences in life. Good sex transports us into ecstasy (a Greek word that means "outside yourself"). And we all want that. We all want to leave the drudgery of the world behind and be moved to a better place, if only for a few moments. The draw of sex is its combination of self-satisfaction and possession at the same time. This is why the Greeks used the word *eros* when they spoke of sexual desire. It is a desire that wants to *possess* the object of its affection.

God's way is self-sacrifice. Any sexual behavior that is focused on my fulfillment and my desires is skirting the edge of possession. Paul tells us to be careful. It is so easy to slip over the edge. What do we tolerate that is laced with *porneias*? Soap opera? Romance novels? Prime-time television? Beer ads? Not telling our children about the sacred rules of sexual conduct? We could all make very long lists, I'm sure. The task of the believer is to reclaim sex under God's banner. It is a lifetime job.

Uncleanness – The Greek is *akatharsia*. This word comes from *kathairo* (we derive the English "catharsis"). Here Paul makes it a negative, so the meaning is "not cleansed". The background of *katharos* is ritual cleansing. It is not the same word that is used for the purity of holiness before God. That word is *hagnos* (it comes from a word meaning "to stand in awe"). Why would Paul speak of ritual cleansing rather than purity of heart? This doesn't seem to make sense. After all, he was not writing to Jews. His audience may not have known all the Jewish laws for ritual purification. And he is trying to press the point of being separated from the sins of the world. Wouldn't he choose *hagnos* rather than *katharos*?

The answer lies in the Old Testament background of the word *katharos*. The equivalent Hebrew word for "cleanse" is *taher*. It is used more than 200 times in the Old Testament. In almost every case, it is about ritual purity. These are the actions that need to be taken before, during and after religious events. They included ritual washing of hands, preparations of sacrifices, prayers and many other details. But the intention of all of these actions is to point us toward God's holiness, not to make us holy. The Bible says over and over that no amount of ritual conformity on our part will ever make us holy and acceptable to God. Only God can clean us up from the inside. God will do the real cleansing. He will wash away all the guilt and all the judgment. He will forgive.

When Paul uses the Greek word *akatharsia*, he is saying that these people have not allowed God to wash them clean. They are still practicing the art of self-justification. They still believe that they can become pure on their own. When we see this connection, the damnation that Paul brings upon his first century audience really hits home now. Our present religious rituals like rote prayers, communion without consecration, baptism without commitment, Easter and Christmas celebrations, attending church and any other actions that we do cannot replace what God has to do if we are to be His people. Without God's cleansing, none of the rest of this matters. With God's cleansing, all of it is a proclamation that we have been washed by our Creator. Either way, it is not about us. Being cleansed today is letting God remove the guilt and sin that has polluted my life. It's a job I can't do for myself.

Paul is condemning those who think they can make it to God their way. But he is also saying more than this. He uses *akatharsia* in a sequence. The sequence is "adultery, fornication, *akatharsia*, lustfulness" – four words that he groups into his comments about sex sins. People who practice the art of self-justification also violate God's sovereignty over their bodies. They believe that they are in control. They believe in the rights of human beings to decide their own fate. Whether it is abortion or intercourse, they think that it's up to them. They have not understood the ritual of consecration to God. So, *akatharsia* also belongs in the "sex sins" group. It is the description of a life that serves itself.

There is still more. Association with those who were impure violated ritual purity. So it is with *akatharsia*. If we associate with those who flaunt God's sovereignty, we are tainted with their impurity. We are unclean by contact and implicit endorsement. If you aren't standing up for God's authority, you are lying down with the unclean. This is why Paul says to the church in Corinth, "If you allow sexual misconduct in your group, all of you share in the guilt and blame". Impurity is a contagious disease. It will spread wherever it is not resisted.

Lasciviousness - the last word Paul uses in this group is *aselgeia*. Since Paul is speaking of sexual issues, here the word means sexual license, that is, sexual excess. To get a picture of what Paul has in mind, we should notice that the same word is used to describe the moral condition of the people in Sodom and Gomorrah. The story of Sodom is found in Genesis. Reading it once will convince you that Paul certainly had insatiable desire for sex in mind when he used this word. The men of Sodom were interested in only one thing – sexual satisfaction. It made no difference to them if the victims were men or women. Their goal was conquest and pleasure.

The judgment of Sodom and Gomorrah has fallen out of favor in today's vocabulary. Perhaps we need to resurrect it. Dr. Patrick Carnes wrote a book called *Out of the Shadows*. It is a study of sexual addiction. He defines this addiction as a fixation on the mood altering experiences of sexual stimulation. The results are impaired thinking, sincere delusion, unmanageable behavior and cyclical acceleration of the required experiences. There are both physiological and psychological factors present in this kind of addiction. Paul tells us that there are spiritual factors as well. Carnes estimates that there are 25 million sexual addicts in the United States. Most of these people never encounter the law. They fight battles with affairs, prostitution, pornography, voyeurism, masturbation, exhibitionism and multiple sexual relationships. If left undiscovered and unrestrained, this road always leads to serious sexual offenses. By God's grace, most addicts never get that far. This is the kind of spiritual warfare that leaves its victims in despair and loneliness. It is gender neutral. Women who can't find the right man in one relationship after another are just as susceptible as men who keep magazines on hand for a quick change in mood. Satan has gained more ground with "socially acceptable" sexual indulgences than with all the murders in the world. Anyone who has ever gone through this brutal battering of the heart and soul will attest to its power.

Paul tells us that those who are on this road are not traveling toward God's kingdom. This thought should strike terror in the hearts of those of us who are nearly helplessly ravaged by sexual compulsion. They already feel a desert of emptiness inside. To be told point-blank that God finds them guilty as charged is nearly a deathblow. A priest I knew once told me that the only thing addiction did was keep him alive until God could rescue him for his hell. The only alternative would have been suicide. Thank God that no sin is beyond His grace to forgive and no soul beyond His power to renew.

Idolatry - Paul leaves behind the group of words concerning sexual sins and moves directly to *eidololatreia*. This is the word for "idolatry" - a combination word made up of the word for servant and the word for an image or representation. The choice of placement in his list is not accidental. All sexual sin is a form of idolatry. Left alone, all sexual sin turns inward, worshipping and serving the insatiable self. It is idolatry in its most subtle form – hidden and never satisfied. It is the idol of "just one more time". This is a logical bridge from a life that lusts.

In the culture of the first century, idols were often constructed as physical images of some god. Certainly Paul has this in mind. But Paul knows that the real power of idolatry is not found in wood or stone. It is found in the allegiance of the heart. So, the word here is not just the word for an idol, it is the word for one who *serves* another god.

The Christian church has made a lot of this word. We are often told about the sins of allowing something other than God to become our first priority. Money is a favorite (for good reason). Power, career, success, material possessions, even other relationships have all been decried for their potential to seduce us. All of these can fall within the scope of idolatry. But I wonder if we have overlooked the subtle elements in our identification of the obvious.

This word is used once in Colossians (3:5) and Ephesians (5:5). In both cases, Paul equates covetousness with *eidololatreia*. In other words, Paul is saying that the essence of serving an idol is the uncontrolled desire to want more – more power, more property, more prestige. It is the desire to be better than others, to take by force or to assert oneself. The Greek is *pleonexia*. It means "greed". We have to think carefully to see why "greed" is the basis of "idol serving". Serving an idol is motivated by the desire to control. Idol worship is either appeasement of a god in order to gain favor or placating a god in order to be granted power. In either case, the motive is to control my own fate for the express purpose of fulfilling my desires. In other words, I serve an idol in order to get what I want. Implied in that effort is the sin of coveting. I don't have enough. I am not satisfied with my current circumstances. I am not content with what God has given me or where He has placed me. So, I turn to my own efforts to get more.

Behind the idol of money or power or success or material wealth or the latest look or the best body is the desire to have more than God's provision. That's why it is idolatry. Not because money, success or a dozen other things are wrong, but because I succumb to the desire to tell God how my life should be lived. It is the essence of greed – to have more than what God knows is the best for me. And the enemy of the best is always "just a little better".

Paul uses "servant of idols" because it bridges the thoughts from sexual sins (which are entirely the result of sexual greed) to the wider scope of all greed – the denial that God knows what He is doing in your life.

Witchcraft - From "idol servant" follows sorcery. The word is *pharmakeia*. Yes, that's right. We get the word "pharmacy" and "pharmaceutical" from this word. The root word has the meaning we would expect – drugs. Witchcraft, sorcery, magic and the occult all used drugs to administer their trade in the first century. It is not much different today. Love potion #9 is still part of magic. Paul says those who make efforts of manipulate and control the world in this way are on the path to hell. Of course, what Patrick Carnes said about sex is no less true about drugs. Mood altering is an attempt to manipulate the reality God has given. It is turning to self-in-control (or out of control, as the case may be) instead of submitting to God in control.

So much has been said about the drug problem that it hardly bears mentioning, except to point out that it was a problem for the Christian church in the first century too. But the issue behind all of these sins, from adultery to *pharmakeia* is the same – not being content with God's provision for life. And the method for solving that desire is also the same for all these sins – self deification – I will be my own god and the world will be the way I want it to be.

Hatred - Of course, whenever we decide that we should run the world and make it suit our tastes, we confront a problem. Other people. That conflict produces the sin called enmity. The Greek is *echthrai*. It comes from the Greek word that means "enemy". It is the conflict that occurs when someone else does exactly what we do while we operate under the principle of self-deification. They want to be god too. And the world only has room for one God. If I have given myself over to sins of pleasure and sins of manipulative control, I will always be confronted with those who don't do what I want them to do. When my way is frustrated, I will experience hatred toward them in the form of jealousy, malice, anger or animosity. Enmity is not a word that we use much today, but we are certainly aware of its results. Civil unrest, racial tension, violence, fraud, genocide, bitterness and slander make the news everyday. One person against another. One group opposed to another. One nation at war with another. All motivated by the need to control. All following the pathway of power. We have met the enemy and he is us. Hatred is the result of too many gods. Two is too many. There is only one God and if we are not serving Him, we will find we harbor hatred for everyone who is not serving us.

Paul expands the meaning of this word with the next five nouns: variance, emulations, wrath, strife and seditions. All descriptions of enemies in conflict.

Variance - *Eris* is the word translated "**variance**". It really means fighting. It is the word for strife and contention. It covers a wide range, from arguing and body language to actual blows. Enemies must be dealt with. God's way is to convert my attitude into submission to God so that an enemy becomes an opportunity for grace. My way is to convert my enemy to submission to me. That usually doesn't happen without force. Too many gods means a battle will result. How many times in your life have you heard (or used) "My way or the highway"? The recipe for strife begins with an attitude of quarreling. Even if you're right, you're wrong. My wife reminds me all the time that it is not the message that counts; it's the tone of the delivery.

Christians are called to show self-sacrifice toward enemies. That can only be done through God's help. It is not "natural". The natural way is the way of *eris*.

Emulations – The word is *zeloi*. It means "to be hot, fervent". We get the word zealot from this Greek root. When it is translated in the positive sense, it means favorable emotion. The Bible tells us to be zealous about God's purposes and God's word. That means we are to have strong feelings about what God wants for us and what He says to us. The Bible also tells us that God is a *jealous* God. This is the word used for that expression. Now you can see that it means that God has intense feelings about you, sin and holiness.

But there is a bad sense of jealousy. In this verse, it is used in the bad sense. There are two ideas here. The first is jealousy. Jealousy is feeling evil intensity toward what appears to be good in someone else. It is the fervent desire to take something away from another. Jealousy is a fire that is only quenched by possession. The implication behind jealousy is self-rule. When I am jealous, I tell myself that what someone else has should really be mine. I am the

---

91

ruler of my world and what I want I get. Jealousy is a sin against God. Why? Because God is the One Who decides the proper distribution of His possessions among His children. He is the rightful Ruler. So, if He gives someone money or power or fame or anything else, it is up to Him. When I decide that what someone else has should be mine, I am telling God that He didn't know what He was doing. I could have run the universe better. I want to be in control to serve myself.

Jealousy brings on malice. Malice is a term used in legal settings today. But it has much wider application. It means to harbor vindictive feelings that express themselves in evil acts and intentions toward someone. You can see why jealousy and malice are connected. When I live according to my rule, jealousy tells me that I deserve to have what you have. As I let that jealousy work in my life, it produces feelings of hatred toward you. My soul burns with the desire for what you have. I start to think about how I can take what you have. And, of course, the only way to take what you have is to act with evil intention toward you. If I discover that I can't take it from you (a reminder that I am not God), then another form of malice takes over. I want to get even. I will become vindictive. You have it but I can't get it. So, I will hurt you some other way. How much evil comes from not acknowledging God's right to place possession in our care.

The consequence of quarrelling, jealousy and malice is **wrath**. The Greek word is *thumoi*. Wrath is not a very good translation here. The word usually translated wrath in the New Testament is *orge*. *Thumoi* is the word for outbursts of anger. It comes from the idea of an explosion, a sudden violent movement. Isn't that exactly what happens when we let the attitude of arguing take over? We fight with words. Then we want to get even. Then, suddenly, we just can't hold it back anymore. We explode.

Once I worked in a juvenile prison. The kids who were sent there by the court came with big attitude problems. They hated the system for catching them. They hated the staff for controlling them. They hated themselves for corrupting them. All of that intensity could erupt at any moment. One day one of the girls sat on a desk in the office taking about her life. She seemed calm and controlled but as she talked about her experiences she suddenly exploded in anger. She smashed her arm through a glass window, blood splattering everywhere. Then she picked up a broken piece and turned toward the staff person. "I just want to kill you", she screamed. That is *thumos* (*thumoi* is the plural).

Rivalries – The next word is *eritheiai*. This is a plural word, just like *thumoi*. "Rivalries" is an old way to translate this word. Today we would say, "self-interest". The picture behind this word is about work. The word describes someone who works of hire but with a purely selfish motive. They are only interested in what's in it for them. Work is a sacred assignment under God's rule, to be carried out with His holiness in mind. *Erithetai* is entirely focused on self-interest, pitting my desires against yours. It is the employee who takes advantage, the partner who defrauds, the company that cheats. Personal gain is more valuable than honesty and self-sacrifice. It is a word that describes the attitude that I am more important than others. "Watching out for Number One" is the motto of this person.

Seditions - Now Paul introduces two words that show how the creation of enemies spills over into God's intention for unity among believers. The first word is *dichostasiai*. It means "division". It comes from two words: *dicha* which means "separate" and *stasis* which means "place". Those who are enemies divide themselves into separate places. They experience dissension. They can't agree so they move away. Even if their separation is not physical, it can be a separation of words, a failure to agree on what they believe. This is *haireseis* (**heresy**). It means "to choose, to have a contrary opinion". It is not *schisma* which is an actual separation but rather a separation in belief that stays within the group but creates antagonism. Sins between individuals become sins between groups, separating and dividing what God intended to be joined. Here we see the pattern of adultery working its way out in the life of an entire assembly of people. God wants harmony, unity and solidarity. Capitulation to the desire for pleasure will lead inevitably to separation. In marriage, it is called divorce. Between groups it is called alienation.

Paul concludes this list with four words that describe the behavioral expression of the inner rage when I want to play god in a world that doesn't belong to me. The first is *phthano* (**envy**). It means "envy, jealousy and malignity at the sight of excellence in others". We translate this word "envy" but it also means "ill-will, malice, jealousy". Why would Paul use this word when he has already used the word *zeloi*, a word that also means "envy"?

The answer is this: *zeloi* is a word that has both a good and a bad sense. It can mean the intense good feelings I have for God and His grace, or it can mean the intense bad feelings I have toward someone that I hate. But *phthonoi* never has a good sense. It is always evil. Just like *eritheiai*, it is explosive. It is the deep feeling of despising someone because you can't control him. It's the "I just can't help it" feeling when you feel real pain because someone else is happy but you aren't. There is a good reason that we say, "Misery loves company". Envy is behind this saying. If I can't be happy, then I don't want you to be happy either.

Murders – The word Paul uses is *phonoi*. It comes from *phonos*. It means murder, but especially slaughter. Lots of killing without mercy or consideration. It might look like killing just for the pleasure of it, but we now know that it is the result of thinking that the world should be what I want it to be no matter what. And when I discover that the world does not bend to my will, the ultimate solution is to destroy what doesn't conform to me.

Thankfully, most of us are not murders. We all agree with Paul that this form of self-in-control is reprehensible and intolerable. But maybe we all haven't seen that murder is connected with a list of sins that goes back to adultery. How can murder be connected to adultery? Adultery is the murder of the "one" unit God made in a marriage. It destroys that unity. It is murder by sex instead of murder by the sword. But it destroys something God made. It destroys God's image in plural – two become one.

Murder destroys God's image in singular. God is very clear about the sacred quality of that image. It is His reflection and the representation of Himself. We do not have the right to erase it.

We can trace the chain of sin. The desire for pleasure (the sins of sex) leads to the desire for power (the sins of control) that leads to the creation of enemies (sins of conflict). The next step in this line of self-deification is the destruction of those who will not submit (sins of subjection).

Drunkenness – The word is *methai*. It comes from a word that means "boundary or limit". The Bible does not tell us that alcohol is forbidden. The decision to drink alcohol is an individual choice to be made before God. This sin is not about consumption. It is about not knowing your limits. Think of it as the sin of going to far. It could be about alcohol, but it doesn't have to be when we consider it in the context of limits. God has placed proper limits on all behavior. Violating those limits is sin. James reminds us the sin is knowing what is right and not doing it. There are limits on drinking but there are also limits on eating, working, spending, talking, driving, choosing, even on thinking. If we see this word in its root sense, we will see that sin is always going beyond the border set by God. Someone once told me that God's rules are like fences. They set the boundaries. What we do inside the fence God leaves up to us. But God puts the fence there to protect us, not to keep us in. There is plenty of freedom inside the fence. There is danger outside. *Methai* is a question of boundary control. If you don't have it, you will be in grave danger. Life inside the fence is blessed, joyful and secure. Life outside is treacherous. You might find someone outside that fence who has decided to be god and doesn't want you in the world.

Finally, Paul ends the list with **revellings**. The Greek word is *komos*. It is the natural extension of the word for drunkenness.

Komos was the word used for festivals in honor of the Roman god Bacchus, the god of wine. At these festivals, men and women exhibited all kinds of "borderless" behavior. Today we call them drunken orgies, but if we knew what the Greek word *orge* really meant, we might have a different view of the party. *Komos* is an apt description of the "party" mentality. Anything goes. It is MTV on Spring Break. You get the picture.

Paul tells us that we have come full circle. What started as a desire for someone else has ended in a disregard for our own limits and the safety and security of everyone else. We have thrown away those moral laws that govern God's universe. He won't forget.

Sins of pleasure lead to sins of power. Sins of power lead to sins of conflict. Sins of conflict lead to sins of subjection.

And sins of subjection lead us to sins of trespass. We trample over God's borders and arrive back where we started – seeking sins of pleasure. It is a vicious cycle. Once you get on board, you will not get off until you stop the train. This train only stops when you die.

Discipline
Direction and Destination

We all know that we need it. We all know the struggle to maintain it. We all know that God expects it. *Discipline*! The process of bringing our lives into alignment with God's purposes and character is a life-long effort. It has peaks and valleys. It is measured by progress and failure. It involves comforting intimacy and distressing repentance. Perhaps Eugene Peterson captured the essence of this never-ending conformity with his title, *A Long Obedience in the Same Direction*. Perhaps discipline is more about the *direction* of my life than it is about the individual steps I take. Of course, steps taken in the *wrong* direction don't lead to the goal of conformity to the image of the Son, so not *any* steps will do. But as long as I am moving in the right direction, discipline seems to be the pathway God provides.

The Bible has a lot to say about discipline. Biblical discipline involves ritual, character, decision-making, prayer, obedience, exhortation, celebration, warnings and examples. God's instructions give us a roadmap for holy living. The map doesn't cover *every* detail (no map does), but it does provide us with enough specifics so that we can be sure of many behaviors and can derive most of the rest. In other words, God doesn't let us flounder around in the dark, trying to live according to some general principle like "love," but never actually knowing precisely what this principle means in action. No, God provides us with exact expectations about life's simplest things, like what to eat, when to worship, how to treat neighbors and strangers, what to say in prayer – and then He gives us real examples of men and women who followed Him and who did not follow Him. God's roadmap is filled with landmarks. If we pay attention to them, we are more than likely to stay on track.

Nevertheless, discipline is a frightening topic. It is frightening because most of us are keenly aware of how far we are from a truly disciplined life. We don't like to open the closet or lift the lid and discover the mess of our inner struggles. But the Bible is a book about *revealing* the truth and that revelation is often quite painful. Apparently pain is part of discipline (as the Hebrew word *musar* clearly indicates). So, let's venture forth, knowing the God confronts and comforts. Let's examine our current behavior. Let's set aside all those wonderful spiritual *words* we claim and look at how we actually live. Let's see if s study of biblical discipline won't bring us to our knees and then lift our faces to see Him smile.

1.

*"Please do not let my lord pay attention to this worthless man, Nabal, for **as his name is**, so is he. Nabal is his name and folly is with him."* 1 Samuel 25:25

Skyboxes

As His Name Is - *khishmo kenhu* says the Hebrew text. It's a phrase about *you* and *me*! I don't mean that we are fools like Nabal. I mean that from a Hebrew perspective, names are not simply linguistic referral devices. Names have *intrinsic* meanings. This fact reveal something very important about the way the Hebrew Scriptures view the world. It's *not* how we see the world, and the difference makes all the difference. If you want to see the world from *God's* point of view, you're going to have to shift your paradigm.

You remember that Greek is a static, analytic language. That means that Greek looks at the world as *things*. Greek language refers to these *things* with nouns, but the nouns themselves have no intrinsic connection to the essence of the thing. In other words, we can refer to a person who resides without legal status in a country as an "illegal alien" or we can modify the wording and change the connotation of the words to "undocumented worker." Both phrases refer to the same person, but they have *different meanings* (Isn't political correctness fascinating?). The words that we use are not *essentially* connected to the thing that they refer to. Think about the shift in meaning of the word "gay" over the last fifty years. Since the Greek world uses words only as *referring* agents, the words themselves can be manipulated without a change in the underlying thing. This is what happens quite often in theology. Liberal theologians change the *words* that refer to the virgin birth or the resurrection but still *refer* to the same thing.

Manipulation of language like this is not possible in Hebrew. Why? Because Hebrew began as pictures, images of what was essential to the object described. When Adam named the animals, he didn't just pull the names out of the air. The names he chose revealed what made that particular animal what it was. The same is true of names for human beings. Nabal isn't just any name. It is a name that describes who Nabal is. He is foolish *as his name says*. So, what's the picture behind the Hebrew N-B-L? It means, "one who is pulled along (controlled) by activity in the house." In other words, this person doesn't see beyond the daily grind. His life revolves around what's happening right now in his home. His world is all about him, and from a Hebrew perspective, that is the essence of a fool. Ah, maybe we're not so far away from Nabal as we would like to think.

Now, notice that the Hebrew noun, Nabal, is really a description of *actions*. It doesn't just refer to a person who happens to be called by this word. It reveals the *actions* of that person. His name can't be disconnected from how he lives. Hebrew is a *verbal* language, focusing its attention on the actions that make up the flow of the world. There are certainly things in the Hebrew world, but what they are is derived from what they *do*. If you want to know the truth about God's world, you have to investigate the *activities* in God's world, not just have a list of nice little boxes to put things in.

Now that you begin to see how different this is, think about something else that is *essentially* Hebrew: God's *name*. God's name is a form of the verb "to be." Let me assure you that God is not sitting in some noun "skybox". He is *active* in creation. That's who He is! And if we are going to be like Him, what do you think that means? That you have the right theology, or that you are *doing* His work in the Kingdom?

2.

*"Forgive us our **debts**, as we also have forgiven our debtors."*
Matthew 6:12

The Price To Pay

Debts – There are only two critical terms in a debt: who and what. Without those two terms, the debt means nothing. So, let's ask the obvious questions. In the Lord's Prayer, whom do I owe and what do I owe? Since the prayer is addressed to God the Father, the answer to the first question is obvious. I owe my debt to God. I am petitioning Him to forgive something that I owe Him. But the answer to the second question requires a bit more thinking.

What debt do I owe to God?

A debt implies that something has been given to me that I am under obligation to return. If you loan me money, I must repay the funds. If I borrow your car, you expect it back. If I borrow your pen, the obligation is not diminished. I need to give you a pen. What I receive, I must return. In Hebrew, this is called "measure for measure." It applied to legal and moral circumstances. An eye for an eye is the same principle as dollar for dollar. So, then, what have I received from God?

Suddenly the curtain is pulled back. The answer is: everything! I am in debt for my breath, my health, my sight, my arms, my protection, my provision, my job, my wife, my home, my children, my mind, my talents, my hopes and dreams. Everything I have is on loan from the Father. Without His benevolence, I do not exist. I owe Him *all that I am*. That is a very difficult debt to repay! Life for life, says that Old Testament. It dawns on me. To repay this debt will require my life. I must give back what He has given. In order to pay this one, I will have to die.

"Forgive me this debt" is my plea to my Creator to let me live without demanding my life in repayment. My status as His debtor will *never* go away. I have no way to repay this debt without dying. If I am to live, He will have to forgive what I owe. And He is willing to do this. That's amazing. Can you imagine what it would be like to forgive someone such a debt? The debtor would be forever grateful, forever humble, forever your voluntary servant in thanksgiving.

Of course, there is a little twist to this story. Forgiveness requires substitution. You see, the record can't be simply erased. I can't take it off the books. If I did, the balance sheet wouldn't balance. The needed capital will have to come from someplace else. It does. God Himself repays. He dies for me.

Is this what you have in mind when you repeat these words? Did you think it was only about "sins"?

3.

*for we do not know **how to pray** as we should, but the Spirit Himself intercedes for us with groanings too deep for words;* Romans 8:26

Now What?

How To Pray – Is this really the problem? Does Paul mean to say that we don't know *how* to pray? It doesn't seem so. Prayer is ultimately about commune with God. It is about all of the emotional, volitional, cognitive and embodied elements that bridge the gap between who I am and who

God is. I don't think I really have any serious concerns about *how* I pray. I know that the Hebrew words cover the range from growling to weeping, from shouting to dancing and from pleading to praising. The real problem is that I don't know *what* to pray. I don't really know what God is doing in the circumstances of my life, so I don't really know what to say that will align my heart with His purposes. I am stuck with the finite version of the eternal plans of God. More often than not, I am at a loss for true perspective.

Someone is sick. What should I pray? Should I pray for healing? What if that is not what God is doing with these circumstances? Someone lost a job. Do I pray for another, or is God teaching something else? At every hand I am confronted with confusion. How can I pray rightly if I do not know the mind of God first? Do I just toss up words and add the "if it is Your will" catch-all at the end? Paul seems to say something else.

First, the Greek phrase does not include the word *pos* (how). Therefore, any translation that *adds* this thought doesn't seem to be correct. There is also no justification for adding the "for" in a translation such as "what to pray *for*." Paul literally says, "because what we may pray as we ought, we do not know." Leon Morris comments: "But we cannot hide behind a plea of ignorance and give up on prayer. Prayer is part of the Christian life. . . We must pray aright, and since we cannot do that, the Spirit comes to our aid." Paul's comment is not an excuse for incapacity. It is a description of our finitude. We don't know *what* to pray because in our brokenness in a broken world we *cannot* know what to pray. Unless God shows up in our prayers, we are simply guessing.

The Greek verb here is *proseuchomai*, the standard New Testament word for praying. It is a general category word, covering all the elements of prayer. Paul isn't saying that we lack insight when it comes to intercession or supplication. He is saying that the human condition leaves us deficient in *all* aspects of prayer. If you have ever struggled in conversation with God, you know that Paul speaks the truth. Prayer is very difficult. Without the Spirit, there is always an awareness of inadequacy in the experience.

A lot of us recognize this problem, but now what? Perhaps it helps to recognize that the Hebrew approach to prayer almost always focuses on praise and blessing for God. In fact, most prayers in the Siddur (the Hebrew prayer book) are filled with blessing and praising God's name, His works and His faithfulness. There seems to be a lot less concern about human needs and supplications. What comes to the forefront is the magnificence and majesty of God. Maybe these prayers don't struggle so much with the issue of incapacity because they start by acknowledging the impossibly wide gap. Furthermore, when the prayers of the Siddur do bring needs before the King of the Universe, the attitude is always focused on the transformation of the supplicant's heart in order to be content with the sovereign will of the King. In other words, the prayer is not so much about what we want God to do as it is about becoming pliable and accepting His purposes. Prayer is real petition, but it focuses on the degree of *my* contentment. God's sovereignty always trumps my desires and I need to absorb that.

Finally, it might be helpful to see that prayer is a duty, not simply a desire. We are commanded to pray. That means we must pray in spite of our feelings about the situation. How easy it is to shed the discipline of prayer when we are discouraged or downtrodden. But prayer is not emotionally based. Prayer is the requirement to talk to Him about it.

"Why didn't you come to me sooner," is God's answer to our hesitancy. We need to make prayer a discipline of life. Once again, this is demonstrated in the Siddur, an aid that begins prayer at the very moment we wake and has prescribed prayers for nearly every activity in the day. Maybe the rabbis knew how quickly we lose sight of God in the hustle and bustle of life, so they built into the training process the constant reminders of Creator conversation. Paul concurs with his exhortation, "Pray without ceasing."

In personal confession, I recognize that I do not know what to pray. That often leads me to not pray, since I can see no way out of the circumstances I face. I don't know what to do, so I don't know what to ask. Not knowing what to ask, I ask nothing at all. But this is a terrible and debilitating mistake and an awful display of arrogance. Who am I to know? The solution to the problem is not asking God to assist me with my solutions. I don't have a solution. Therefore, I am left with pouring out my heart-felt struggle *without an answer*. That opens the door for the Spirit. All I have really done is come to the Father with these words on my lips: "I do not know what to pray, Father, but I know who You are. Let my heart be molded to Your purposes. That is enough for me."

This isn't the end of the story, but it is a beginning.

4.

*The sorrows of those who have bartered for another god will be **multiplied*** Psalm 16:4

Turning Up The Volume

Multiplied – Life without the Lord is increasingly miserable.

That's the biblical message. It sometimes doesn't appear that way. After all, the systems of this world support rebellion against God, rewarding those who actively engage in disobedience. But, as the Bible says, the wicked will not prevail. Their end is assured, and it is assuredly terrible. The psalmist warns us not to envy the wicked for they have no future. In this verse, God speaks about judgment. Serving false gods will result in turning up the volume. Sorrows will be multiplied.

If you read this in Hebrew, you would quickly see that the first word in the phrase is *ravah*, a verb that means "to be many, to be abundant, to increase." This is the emphasis of the sentence. "Many" more sorrows follow idolatry. We might notice that absence of sorrow isn't in the picture. Everyone has sorrow. That's what it means to be in a broken world. *Atsav* was introduced into this world with the original decision to determine life's direction without God's input (Genesis 3). Sorrow is a part of our existence. In this poem, the word is *'atstsevet*. It isn't about anxiety or toil. It's about anticipated pain! Derived from *atsav*, this word is only found in Hebrew poetry. It implies the grief that comes from fear of punishment. It isn't about the actual pain itself. It's about the emotional suffering and torment that comes from knowing you deserve to be disciplined. The distinction is important.

In this world, both the wicked and the righteous struggle with *atsav*. Life isn't right. In its broken state, bad things happen to everyone. We all toil. We all suffer. We all fall under the grist mill of the enemy. God does not promise that the righteous will somehow be exempt from life on this planet. But He does promise redemption, reinforcements and deliverance. And He promises justice.

Not so for the wicked. Those who serve other gods can expect the sorrow that we all experience to be increased. Why? Does God say, "I'll get you?" No, God weeps over the lost and desires all to turn to Him. The reason that sorrows are multiplied is built into the consequences of idolatry. An idol cannot hear me. An idol cannot respond to me. An idol offers me nothing but mute frustration. Being left to fend for myself is a natural and inevitable consequence of serving a dead god. The living God does not have to take any steps to actively increase the emotional stress and fear of those who refuse to obey Him. They do it to themselves.

Notice that this verse does not say, "I will increase their sorrows." All that is required is that God *withdraw* His grace and mercy. The broken world will do the rest. Whenever men and women are out of alignment with God, the world has its way with them. And in this world, fear holds all those captive who do not serve the living God.

Perhaps you know someone whose sorrows are being multiplied. Perhaps a word from the psalmist is what they really need. Life is broken, but God's people are not.

5.

*For the word of God is **living** and active and sharper than any two-edged sword, and piercing as far as the division of soul and spirit, of both joints and marrow, and able to judge the thoughts and intentions of the heart.* Hebrews 4:12

Embodiment

Living - Is the Bible a *living* Word for you? This is not a trivial question. The Bible is not like other books. There are other books that inspire. There are others books that challenge, encourage, command, discipline and exhort. None of these factors are unique to Scripture. What makes the Bible the *living* Word? It communicates God's will to us. And since God's will for us is *life*, His Word, in any form, brings life with it. It is *zoe* (alive, living, life-filled).

The Greeks did not usually use this word, *zoe*, when they spoke about ordinary life. They used *bios* (our root for "biology"). For the Greeks, *bios* was about life right here, the day-to-day activities that made up what we experience as being alive. A recounting of present life is called a *biographe* (literally "life-writing"). But the Greeks did have a use for *zoe*. Unless we understand how they thought about *zoe*, we will not see the startling claim in this verse.

Greek metaphysics is built around the duality of the material and the spiritual. OK, I know, that was a bit scholarly. What it means is that the Greeks thought of existence in terms of two levels. One was the level of the material world, where all the stuff we see and deal with exists. The other was the spiritual world, where the divine resides with Truth, Beauty and Goodness. This dual nature of reality has affected Western civilization for thousands of years. In fact, it is the fundamental philosophical principle behind the Christian idea of getting to heaven. Our proclamation of "escape" from this world, whether through divine intervention, rapture, other-worldly orientation or a heavenly gate pass, is really the affirmation that the "spiritual" world is the preferred existence and getting out of here is the real goal. "Where will you go if you die tonight?" is an evangelistic approach that is rooted in Greek metaphysics. The assumption is that getting to heaven is the goal of Christian belief. It sounds nice. Who wouldn't want to leave all their problems behind? But it's not biblical. Too bad!

So, the Greek term *zoe* refers to what we would call "the force." *Zoe* is the life-animating principle that comes from the realm of the divine, empowers existence in the material world, and at death, returns to the realm of the spirit. *Bios* is where I have to struggle with my individual existence, but *zoe* is my true home, apart from this valley of tears, existing blissfully in the world of the divine. Of course, in the realm of *zoe*, there are no particular individuals. We all flow back into the life-force. In this world, where *bios* reigns, we are intrinsically *unfulfilled*. We can never reach our true state of oneness with the divine because we are "trapped" in a material body that belongs in a material world. In order to reach fulfillment (and perfection), we must escape from this realm and leave the material world behind. Its very presence constrains us. In the realm of *zoe* we are freed from the material and can exist as pure spirit, operating under the banner of *nous*, reason alone. For the Greeks, the world is an evil prison keeping us from being the truly rational beings we were meant to be.

This dualism is still with us. Every time you hear someone speak about the evil world, the bliss of heaven, the desire to depart, the anticipation of the rapture or anything that suggests that our purpose is departure, you are probably treading on Greek philosophy. It has been part of the church since the third century. But it is *not* found in the Bible.

The author of Hebrews calls the Word of God "living." He uses *zoe*. With all this Greek metaphysics in the background, why would he use such a loaded term? The answer is that he uses the term as it is found in the Septuagint, where it is influenced by the Hebrew concept of *nephesh*. But *nephesh* is not separate from physical life. In fact, it is essentially linked to life as we know it in this world. Why? Because the world is the creation of God and it is *good*! There is no dualism, no separation between spiritual and physical. God created the world a wonderful, full, significant place where we are to discover His glory in our embodiment. Getting to heaven is definitely *not* the goal! Enjoying His Kingdom on earth, and seeing it manifest, is the goal. That's why Yeshua prays that we will *not* be taken out of this world. We are to experience life in all its fullness right here. Yes, it's broken. Sin has corrupted this place. But it is not trashed. It is not evil. It is under the influence of evil, but it is to be redeemed. Leaving is not an option if you want to be where God is active.

There is one more important step in recovering the meaning of this word in this verse. *Nephesh* is all of me, all homogenized together. I am not body-mind-soul. I am the manifestation of God's breath embodied. And that means that I am entirely under His sovereignty. Life does not belong to me. It belongs to Him. He gives it as a *loan* to me. Unlike the Greek concept, I am not on a path to ascend to my true calling in the spirit world. I am me right here, breathing the *nephesh hayyah* that God has given me, designed to do His will on this earth.

What does this tell us about *zoe* in Hebrews 4:12? God's Word is living (*zoe*) because it *embodies* God's character in active declaration. It is the manifestation of who He is. It has the same quality as *nephesh*. It is totally under His control. It is His gift. It is good. And it is designed for this world. God's Word is God embodied in language. When you read it, you are in the presence of God, filling your thoughts, words and deeds with His character clothed in human communication.

6.

*"and I will **cut** him **off** from among My people. So you will know that I am YHWH."* Ezekiel 14:8

Living Hell

Cut Off – The Hebrew phrase that describes acknowledging my sin as the first step in repentance is *ha-karat ha-chet*. Literally, this is "the sin that cuts off." These words tell us that unless and until a man realizes that God *cuts off* relationship over sin, that man will never have the motivation or the discipline to repent. Doesn't that seem obvious? It should, but for some reason we have entertain a theological seduction that teaches us that God *overlooks* our sins because He is so filled with grace and forgiveness. We really don't believe sin is such a serious issue, especially after we have been "saved." We think that Yeshua covered it all, and now all we need to do is try as best we can while grace smoothes over the rough spots.

Let's look at Ezekiel again. "Anyone of the house of Israel . . who separates himself from Me, sets up idols in his heart, puts right before his face the stumbling blocks of his iniquity, and then comes to . . inquire of Me . . . I will cut him off." Wait! This verse is for us, not those wretched pagans. We are the house of Israel. Have we set up idols in our hearts? Forget the usual stuff – power, fame and fortune. How about the day of the week? Have we made an idol (something that opposes and deposes God) of a particular day - a day God didn't endorse? How about honor? Do we honor parents? Do we truly believe that those who have walked longer with God have something important to teach us? Or are we the Disney generation where only children are able to save the world? Have we made idols of the schedule, the day-timer? Is shopping more important than being or television the solution to relationship struggles?

And what about the iniquity shoved in God's face? Are we immune to the Spirit's prompting because we have established a pattern of disobedience and *expect* God to understand? Are we caught in a repeated sinful pattern that we can't break because we really don't want to? Have we *rationalized* our actions, transforming us from perpetrators to victims? Do we play the blame game? Are we stumbling over the same blocks because we refuse to move them out of the way?

God says He will cut that man off from His people. This is the same word used to establish a covenant. It's about as serious as you can get. If blood is shed to cut the covenant, blood will be shed to remove someone from the covenant. Why would God do such a terrible thing? He tells us. "So you will know that I am YHWH." Sometimes we don't know God until we see that He will *not* be compromised, diminished or toyed with. God says He will set His face against such a man. Go ask Cain what that means. It is living hell – to be alive without God is to starve the soul to death. It's wandering without home or direction.

We will not repent until we confront the hideousness of our sins. Sometimes God is gracious and He does not allow us to see the full scope of our iniquity. Sometimes He isn't quite so gentle. Sometimes it takes blood before we can truly say, "My sin is every before me" (Psalm 51:3).

I don't want to be cut off. But I know that I throw stumbling blocks before the Lord and call them excuses. I know immediately when I am playing the game. I do all that I can to avoid acknowledging my sin. But that behavior is a fool's errand. Without *ha-karat ha-chet* I am in terrible danger. God asks me to return to Him. The first step is admitting that I left.

7.

Dedicate *a youth according to what his way dictates; even when he is old, he will not depart from it.* Proverbs 22:6 (NIV)

My Way Or The Highway

Dedicate – Solomon was a very wise man. His wisdom penetrated the essence of things. His sayings often reveal what we do *not* see on the surface. So, when we read this *mashal* (Hebrew – proverb), we should be careful not to think of it as merely commonsense. Why would Solomon bother to tell us that you can discipline a child to do what you want? That's obvious. The King James idea of "training a child" sends us in the wrong direction. Proverbs is not a book for parents. It's a book for youth. This *mashal* isn't about making a child follow a path determined by parents. It's about directing the child in a path essential to who the child is.

The imperative *chanok* (dedicate) means "to start the youth off with a strong and perhaps even religious commitment to a certain course of action."[25] But what course of action? Waltke writes "[the child] must be assessed individually to design personally the appropriate moral initiative." In other words, the course of action is determined according to the individual makeup of the child. It is tailor-made to fit the essential character of the child. "One rule fits all" is *not* the process Solomon endorses. It can't be "My way or the highway." That isn't what Solomon (or God) has in mind here.

OK, so it's not about uniform rules. It's about unique, individual courses of action. Does that mean parents have different "rules" for each child? No, you missed the point. It's **not about rules!** It's about parental dedication to understand your child so deeply that you see what the child was born to be – and then designing a course of action to allow the child to become what God designed into her. God

---

[25] Waltke, *Proverbs*, Vol. 2, p. 204.

designed each of us to fit perfectly into His delightful plan for creation. Parents have the responsibility to discern what God has in mind for their children and do everything they can to bring that about. When they set a child on a course of action that is in alignment with the way the child is designed by God, the child will never depart from it. "Born to be me" is the operating principle.

So, if you have children, are you able to answer this question: Do you know (from God's perspective) what your children were born to be? If you don't, how can you possibly fulfill the role of parent according to God's design. If you don't know who your child was born to be, you are more than likely to send that child down *your* path, not God's path. And when they are older, they will depart from it because it wasn't who they were.

This is *not* commonsense! This is godly instruction. It is dedication to "what his way dictates," not what you desire. It's action *after* homework. And homework for parents is all about God's design for your child, not your design.

8.

For even though they knew God, they did not honor Him as God or
*give thanks; but they became futile in their speculations, and their **foolish heart** was darkened.* Romans 1:21

Straight-line Depreciation

Foolish Heart – Are you sitting down? You might want to before we examine connections between 1000 years of Christian teaching and the current condition of our world. They aren't connections that we want to see. Perhaps you will be able to convince me that I am mistaken. But like

Paul, I am concerned. Some time ago I stood at the Western Wall of the Temple Mount in Jerusalem and wept. I went there to pray, but there were no words to speak. I was simply crushed by the enormous despair in our world. I don't mean that I saw despair in those who were at the Wall. They celebrated God. What struck me was the awareness that the Church I know has contributed a great deal to this sense of hopelessness, in spite of all its words to the contrary. It is simply not possible to continue to refuse to honor God as God, the way in which He reveals Himself, and expect to walk away unscathed. So, here are some straight-line depreciation ideas to consider. These things bother me. Maybe I'm wrong about them, but if I'm not, what does that mean for you in the next year?

1. For centuries the Church taught that women were not equal with men. Of course, theologians claimed *ontological* equality, but in practice they treated women as weaker, more easily seduced, less disciplined, less capable of leadership or other roles within the Body. These men claimed God divinely relegated women to submission to their husbands. It doesn't really matter what theological manipulations were needed to promote such an idea, the result has been a general disregard for the full humanity of women, encouraged by the culture and tacitly endorsed by the Church. Recently a survey shows that violence toward women in the media is up more than 100%. The world is filled with sex slavery, pornography, abuse, rape and gender bias. I believe this is a straight-line result of a failure to honor God's Word in Genesis and to give Him thanks for His good creation. The Church refuses to acknowledge that God made women priests because they impose Greek thinking on the text. This is a colossal failure to read the text with Hebrew eyes. Today, this issue stands at the forefront of the Christian worldview as the

greatest oppression since the Inquisition. Until it is confronted as hypocrisy, arrogance and sin, the Church has nothing to say to women.

2. The early church fathers introduced the idea of the "new" Israel, a spiritual replacement of God's elect people. Political opportunity, theological hubris, anti-Semitism and other forces conspired to promote what is now the standard, unquestioned theological position of every Protestant denomination and the Catholic Church. This declaration marginalized the people of Israel, obscured or denied their unique place in God's government and shifted the outlook of the Church from an Hebraic to a Greek worldview. The result has been more than one Holocaust. Centuries of disregard for God's people led to the systematic expunging of everything Jewish from Christian thinking. There is a straight-line between this failure to honor God as He revealed Himself and the current collapse of any significant influence of the Church on culture. Look around you. Has the Church stood in solidarity with its Jewish brothers? Has the Church done anything of real significance to stem the tide of immoral, heretical, apostate behavior *even* in its own ranks? Is the Church anything more than a "religious" reflection of cultural values? What can we say to the world when we are responsible for centuries of hatred, violence and rejection of God's people and God's word given to His people?

3. Christianity today is the syncretism of political, economic, social and epistemological views that are not based in the Word of God. Replacement theology did more than promote the supremacy of the Church. It broke the continuity of the culture of God's people. By the end of the second century, the beliefs and practices of Yeshua and his disciples had been

eliminated from the *newly invented* religion of Christianity. Perhaps the reason we read the book of Acts and wonder why our churches do not exhibit such power and persuasion has more to do with our systematic denial of the Hebraic worldview than anything else. We Christians are the apostates. We left the God of Israel behind in our pursuit of power, programs and promises. We converted Israel into a religion of our own making. Of course, most Christian believers today have no idea of the heretical history behind their form of worship, but this much they do know: Something is terribly wrong. Something vital is missing. There is a straight-line between the ignorance, denial and rejection of a Torah-based lifestyle and the insipid, vacuous, frantic romanticism of Christians. A Jew without Torah is obsolete. A Christian without Torah is a hypocrite.

It's worth noting that Paul uses the singular "foolish heart" in this verse. We would have expected "hearts," one for each person. But Paul tells us that they participated in *one* morally mistaken discernment. They were as one in their vain attempt to replace the God of Scripture with their own invention. I wonder if we Christians haven't arrived at the same singular place.

Most people can't remember more than three important things at the same time, so we will stop here. Paul laid a challenge before the Roman followers of Yeshua in his proclamation of the deterioration of their culture. That challenge was simple: Will you follow the pathway of those who deny the God of Israel as He revealed Himself, who refuse to thank Him for His choice of one people to bring all the world to His feet, who pretend that their endless speculations are a substitute for His revealed truth **OR** will you acknowledge Him as He is, honor Him and thank Him by repenting of your hubris and returning to His revealed ways.

Perhaps these three straight-line consequences will cause you to reconsider how you will live. Women, the Church and the Torah community – just these three. It's probably enough.

9.

*they cast lots for their duties, all alike, the small as well as the great, the teacher as well as the **pupil**.* 1 Chronicles 25:8

To Learn

Pupil – What does it mean to learn the Scriptures? Just stop a minute and think about your definition of learning. What characteristics describe a learner – a pupil? Did you include attentive study, memorization, understanding and apprehension? Is the focus of your idea of learning cognitive or experiential? Most of us in this Greek-based worldview think of learning in cognitive terms. We think about gathering facts, understanding problems, drawing conclusions and developing a storehouse of information. In other words, in our world it's possible to learn without ever actually doing anything with the information.

But this is impossible in Hebrew. The word "pupil" is *talmiyd* (singular). You will recognize the similarity with the word Talmud, the collection of oral instruction in Judaism. The word for pupil comes from the verb *lamad*. This verb appears sixteen times in Deuteronomy, usually translated at "teach" or "learn." Are the instructions in Deuteronomy intended to be cognitive collections of facts? Are we supposed to learn God's commandments (Torah) so that we can recite them during a scholarship contest? The same verb shows up in Proverbs 5:13, a verse that gives us a very good picture of the opposite of *lamad*. You'll notice that the emphasis of the verse is about obedience, not information. In fact, the etymological background of *lamad* is to chastise, to discipline even with the rod. Believe me, this is not about beating the facts into you.

A pupil of Scripture in one who bends his will toward God's instruction. Without obedience, nothing is learned. No matter how many times I tell my horse to move to the left when I pull on the reins, if the horse does not obey, no instruction has occurred. This is why it isn't possible to deepen my relationship with God until I learn – and obey - the lesson He has for me today.

One more Scripture example cements the concept (a mental activity). Jeremiah 12:16 says, "And it shall come to pass, if they will diligently learn the ways of my people." The phrase "diligently learn" is really the verb *lamad* repeated twice (*eemlamod yilmedoo*). It is to "learn learn." The Hebrew motto for learning is "Just do it!"

Are you a *talmiyd*? Yeshua called twelve men to be his *talmiydim*. They could not be pupils without being disciples and they could not be disciples without copying his life. "By this they will know that you are my disciples; that you love one another as I have loved you." Making it real, that's what it means to learn.

10.

*I waited, waited for YHWH; And He **inclined** to me, and heard my cry.* Psalm 40:2 (Hebrew Text)

Fish and Snakes

Inclined – *Natah. Nun-Tet-Hey.* That's how you spell this Hebrew verb. The picture? What is revealed (what comes) from life surrounded. Actually, the pictures are fish darting through water (life activity) and a snake coiled around something (surround). OK? So, consider this imagery and ask yourself, "Does God surround my life?" If He doesn't, do you think He will incline toward you?

The verb means more than incline. It means to stretch forth, to bend toward, to pay attention to, to establish, to turn toward, to show _hesed_ toward someone. As God *stretches forth* the heavens, we live under His sheltering sky. He is our Father. He bends toward His children. When our lives are surrounded by His _hesed_, we are cared for. He puts His arms around us and listens to us. The doubled verb (to wait) indicates an attitude of patience on behalf of the psalmist. While God has all the time necessary to accomplish His purposes, we tend to expect His purposes to be completed within our temporal frame. The psalmist reminds us that a double portion of waiting is needed if we are to enjoy God's attention. God is never in a hurry. The state of haste in our lives often runs right past His plans. He pays attention to those who exercise the spiritual discipline of expectant hopefulness since this discipline demonstrates trust in His word.

We all want God to bend toward us. We all want His undivided attention. In fact, we often *press* Him to respond. We are like those people in an elevator who keep pushing the button when the door doesn't close fast enough. Yeshua reminds us that our frenzy for answers displays an attitude of anxiety inconsistent with the _hesed_ of the Lord. Seeking the Kingdom is a corollary of rowing with hope.

If we wait patiently for YHWH and row with the expectation of His fatherly attention, then no decision we make can be a mistake. When we row in alignment, we follow His exhibition of trustworthiness. When we row off course, He guides us back with gentle corrections or chastisement. Either way, we can't miss the final goal. The trick is simply to wait until He turns toward us.

Patience is more than a virtue. It is a necessary component of living the biblical worldview. A man without patience is a man without a word from the Lord. Such a man has accelerated past the next turn in life, moving too fast to see the road signs of warning. Rush hour is a symptom of self-importance. *Natah* surrounds. Its direction is a circle. Slowing down does not prevent getting to the goal. It just makes the circumnavigation much more pleasant.

11.

The fruit of the righteous is a tree of life, and he who is wise ***wins*** *souls.* Proverbs 11:30

Altar Calls

Wins – Of course, we imagine that this verse is a congratulatory pat on the back for those who make the effort to bring others into the Kingdom. We think this verse is motivation for attending evangelism classes, passing out tracts and asking people where they think they will go after they die. Isn't that what it says? If we are really wise, in a spiritual sort of way, we will *win* souls for the Lord.

Ah, but not quite. The context of this verse isn't about getting to heaven at all. It's about being a prudent manager of the assets God gives you so that in times of trouble you will not be poverty-stricken. Read the surrounding verses.

A generous man will prosper. The diligent seeks good favor. The fool has troubles in his house. Discipline and knowledge go together. The Lord hates the perverse. Blessed is the man who makes his goods available to others (even at a price). No, there's no soul-winning here. There's *living* God's way so that we can manage in the broken world. This proverb fits right into the instructions about taking care of what God gives. If you want to experience a tree of life, then be righteous. In the process you will save the lives of many because you will have the assets needed to do so.

The Hebrew verb is *laqah*. It covers the umbrella from seizing and grasping to acquiring, obeying, carrying away and buying. If it is translated "wins," it certainly doesn't have the *eternal* in mind. This verb describes real-time, down-to-earth management. When we realize that Hebrew evangelism is first and foremost about a distinctive lifestyle and the magnetic attraction God promises when we adopt that lifestyle, then we can disconnect from the Greek idea of dragging people into the Kingdom by their epistemological hair. It's not about what you know or how you know it (that's epistemology). It's about what you do in response to the question, "What does God demand of me?" In other words, evangelism is not first on the list of spiritual exercises. In fact, we might even say that it isn't on the list at all. Why? Because God promises to draw those outside the Kingdom to the Kingdom when we are living in Kingdom ways. We are God's magnets, not His bullhorns. There is absolutely no point in recruiting people for the Kingdom if Kingdom activities aren't present in the assembly. That's the difference between a membership drive and a magnetic attraction. We obey. God attracts. But it's an electromagnet. Obedience is the juice that makes it work. Stop obeying and the power turns off. Result: No magnet.

A few days ago Michael noted that his Jewish neighbors are happy to tell him about how they live, but they almost never come to his door to ask him to join them. Conversely, other religious groups seem to show up every week, passing out pamphlets and thumping their Bibles. Why don't Jews engage in that sort of active evangelism? Ah, because they understand that only God draws. All they are asked to do is *live* His way so that when God draws there is someplace for the orbiting proselyte to land.

You can look at it this way. God's air traffic controller is looking for a field to bring in those who want to land in His ways. The evangelism question is not "Who have you asked?" but rather "How well prepared is your field?"

13.

*For God has not given us a spirit of timidity, but of **power** and love and discipline.* 2 Timothy 1:7

Reassessment

Power - God gives me *dunamis*. And what does "power" mean to me? It means ability, capacity, vigor, strength and will. The basis of our words "dynamite" and "dynamic" come from this Greek root. Explosive ability is usually what we think. But when we look at the Hebrew connection, the picture gets a lot fuzzier. When the translators of the LXX tried to find an equivalent for *dunamis*, they came up with quite a list. *Hayil* is used to describe strength, wealth or an army. This is influence, whether financially, numerically or militarily. By the way, the same word is used to describe judging righteously. Another alternative is *lo hassiyr*. This means not lacking, not being deficient or not having poor quality. Not exactly concepts that we naturally associate with power, but obviously part of the Hebrew view of life.

Then there's *yatsa*, a verb that means to go out and come in, or to cause to go out and come in. This verb also carries the idea of bringing forth vegetation and *feelings*. But the LXX isn't done. There is still *'alah* (to ascend, to take away, to offer) and *tsava* (to wage war, to muster for war, to serve). Quite a range. Apparently the Hebrew idea of being able covers a much larger context than our thinking about power.

So when Paul says that God has given us a spirit of power, what Hebrew ideas does he have in mind? Of course, he is using the Greek word, so some of his thoughts are tied to the ideas of capacity, strength and will, but notice how these ideas are played out in the Hebrew culture. Strength finds a home with the general idea of influence. It isn't limited to physical prowess. It is found wherever someone has influence over another, no matter what the basis for that influence. Power is also tied to sufficiency. In a culture where subsistence was a daily issue, power meant not lacking food, shelter and the basics of life. On this scale, *everyone* reading these words is powerful. Hebrew also connects power with the ability to come and go. Ancient cultures were very familiar with slavery, vassal treaties and limitations of movement. We may have forgotten these issues but most of the world has not. Power means being able to move at your own will. It also means being able to express your own feelings, something that you only did with potentially disastrous consequences in a world dominated by emperors and kings. The connection to war is obvious, but maybe not quite so apparent is the connection to *'alah* (to ascend, to take away). This is a verb of sacrifices and offering. What is power if it is not the ability to remove guilt. A sacrifice is power in the most important sense.

Now apply these to Paul's remark to Timothy. Suddenly the concept of power expands significantly. Suddenly we see that our privileged lives of sufficiency, political freedom, influence and expression of feelings are *power*. We discover one other, most important, element. The ability to have our guilt removed through sacrifice is the ultimate expression of power. You never knew you were so well equipped.

13.

*For the word is very near to you, in your mouth and in your heart, that you may **do** it.* Deuteronomy 30:14

Moses Lied

Do – "Evil is not man's ultimate problem. Man's ultimate problem is his relation to God."[26] We might need to read this line from Heschel a few more times. It underscores the difference between the Bible and all other ethical systems. The Bible is a guide to repairing the relationship with God. Actually, it is more accurate to say that the Bible is God's manual about repairing our relationship with Him. It is not an ethical system for overcoming evil. In fact, the Bible doesn't even *explain* the existence of evil. Such an explanation is simply not important. What is important is God's pursuit of Man, His desire for fellowship with us and the amazing steps He has taken to repair this breach. No follower of the King could deny this.

But there is a reciprocal action. God's pursuit of Man is to be reflected in our obedience. He loves first so that we might love second. He chooses us so that we might choose Him. He acts on our behalf so that we might act on His behalf. In other words, the Bible *expects* us to fulfill God's instructions for living. It *assumes* that we are perfectly able to do so. In fact, it *requires* us to pursue Him just as He pursued us.

---

[26] Abraham Heschel, *God In Search Of Man*, p. 376

Moses stood before the people. He delivered God's final instructions before crossing the Jordan. "All of you were born with a sinful nature. You are all sinners, you are all guilty because Adam fell and everyone since then is the product of a sinful constitution. The Law only demonstrates how miserable you are since it isn't possible for you to keep it. That's why I am giving you these holy instructions today, to remind you that you are helpless and hopeless before the Lord. You will never be anything but a sinner until God rescues you." What? That's not what Moses said! He said that God's instructions for righteous living are not only "not too difficult," they are so close to you that you are fully capable of *doing them*. The Hebrew phrase *la-asoto* (you may do it) surrounds the verb *asah*, the verb of simple practical action. More than 1,000 times, it is translated "do." Another 653 times it is translated "make." There is nothing about this verb that suggests we are incapable of completing the action required. In fact, just the opposite it true. The Bible *assumes we are able to do what God asks*.

Moses didn't lie. There is nothing about being human that *prevents* us from doing good except our choice not to obey. Oh, that's a big problem, for sure, but it isn't an inherent problem. It doesn't begin with a corrupt constitution. It begins when I choose to listen to myself. There are two impulses in a man. The one he feeds will dominate him. "There is always an opportunity to do a mitzvah [good deed], and precious is life because at all times and in all places we are able to do His will. This is why despair is alien to Jewish faith."[27]

---

[27] Abraham Heschel, *God In Search Of Man*, p. 378

14.

*And the **salvation** of the righteous is of YHWH; He is their strength in the time of trouble.* Psalm 37:39

What Time Is It?

Salvation – What time is it in your life? Is it a time of trouble? If it is, then the psalmist has a perfect word for you: *teshu'ah* – deliverance!

Let's slow down for a moment and consider *when teshu'ah* comes into effect. Does the psalmist promise deliverance *after* your life is over? Does he proclaim the rescue from YHWH *after* you have run the course? Does he promise that you will have safety *after* you leave this valley of tears? NO! He says that the rescue of YHWH will be experienced *in the time of trouble*, here, now, when it matters. Rescue isn't for the afterlife. Rescue is during life. My time of trouble won't occur when I am safely tucked away in heaven. My time of trouble is right here, in the midst of the storm, in the life of chaos and hurt, in the world under the influence of *yetzer ha'ra*. If God can't rescue me here, if God *won't* rescue me now, then salvation isn't what it needs to be. You and I need help when it matters, not after we are six feet under.

There are times when I am afraid to go to sleep. It's irrational, I know, but that doesn't take away my fear. I am afraid because I know that I have been disobedient. I know that I haven't lived up to my desire to serve Him faithfully and completely. I know that in times of trouble, I have failed. I am afraid to go to sleep because I don't want this moment to be the end. I want to start again tomorrow and have another chance to demonstrate that I really do love Him and I really can be as holy as He wishes me to be. In my time of trouble, I need safety (*teshu'ah*). I need to close my eyes knowing that He loves me even when I fail and that if I wake, He will have trusted me to pick up my cross and follow Him once more.

There are times when I feel overwhelmed with the demands and the complexity of life. There are times when it just seems too much for me. I want to run away from it all. In those times of trouble, I need deliverance (*teshu'ah*). I need to see the simple path of faithful obedience that will take me just one step further down the road. I need deliverance from the distractions of devotion to Him so that my next step is illuminated. I need to be delivered from the preoccupation of planning in order that I might walk in His ways.

There are times when the valley of the shadow of death presses in upon me. When my experience is filled with pain and sorrow, I need rescue (*teshu'ah*). I need the strong arm of the Lord to do the fighting for me. I am exhausted and battle-worn. The sword is too heavy for me to lift today. I need the shelter of His strength while I recover.

What time is it? Perhaps it is time for *teshu'ah* for you.

15.

*For the word of the cross is **foolishness** to those who are perishing, but to us who are being saved it is the power of God.* 1 Corinthians 1:18

Stupid Or Resistant?

Foolishness – I read the footnotes. Footnotes often contain bits of information that are essential for understanding the author's method and meaning. For example, R. T. France has this tiny little footnote on page 430 of his 1169 page commentary on Matthew. "exegesis, here as everywhere, must proceed from the Greek text as we have it." That seems harmless enough, doesn't it? But France uses this statement to dismiss the idea that Matthew 11:12 (a very controversial verse) should be understood from an Hebraic perspective, not a Greek one. The footnote reveals his predisposition.

Unfortunately, biblical authors didn't use footnotes. They didn't use *any* of the modern stylistic markers or punctuation that would help us decipher their meanings. So we have to do a lot more work when we want to understand them.

This verse from Paul's letter to the Corinthians is a case where modern linguistic meanings must be replaced with much more ancient meanings. Contemporary cultural meanings of "foolish" stem from the Greek connection of *moria* with its root *moros*, that is, deficiency, especially mental dullness. If we read this verse with the meaning from classical Greek, then it looks as if Paul is saying that the message of the cross appears *stupid* to those who are being destroyed, lost or ruined (perishing = *apollumi*). But that hardly makes any sense at all. The message of the cross should be the most important thing these people can ever hear. It should be anything but stupid since it is the way of escape from their impending doom. It should be *brilliant insight* and *amazing grace*. Clearly, Paul cannot mean *moria* in the classical Greek sense.

What we discover is that Paul uses *moria* as a summary of the Hebrew view of foolishness. In the Hebrew view, foolishness is not associated with mental dullness. It is associated with lack of the true knowledge of God because of *hardness of heart*. In other words, foolishness is practical atheism. It is living on the basis that there is no God in charge of life. It actually doesn't matter what I *say* about God's existence. If I live as if God doesn't matter to me, I am a fool. With this in mind, the message of the cross is *not* salvation. It is submission! Those whose lives are characterized by practical atheism find the message of submission to be utterly opposed to their behavior. To them, submission is the denial of everything they hold dear. Submission is the antithesis of their values. Consequently, it is considered false and even immoral. The man who believes that he is in charge of his own destiny rejects God's claim as completely impractical illusion.

Once again we discover that understanding Paul requires examination of the Jewish-Hebrew background of his thought. And once again we see that Paul's thought is grounded in *what we do*, not what we say. If we live as though God's directions for life do not matter, we are foolish in the worst sense of the word. We are hopelessly destroying ourselves in our efforts to make up our own rules. Our resistance is only a symptom of a deeper rebellion against God's claim of sovereignty and ownership. To refuse to submit is to deny the power of the cross, a symbol not of forgiveness but of obedience unto death.

16.

*Submit your neck to her **yoke**, that your mind may accept her teaching. For she is close to those who seek her, and the one who is in earnest finds her.* Sirach 51:26

A Burden Accepted

Yoke – On this day when the ancient world celebrated the renewal and return of the fertility gods, a day that

Christianity has adopted into its own calendar for reasons buried in church history, it might do us some good to look at a verse not found in our usual Bibles but nevertheless, apparently on the mind of Yeshua. The parallel is Matthew 11:29 ("Take My yoke upon you and learn from Me, for I am gentle and humble in heart, and you will find rest for your souls"). Of course, we know that that last part of this teaching from Yeshua cites a passage from the prophet Jeremiah. But we might not realize that the first part of this statement parallels passages in Proverbs and in Sirach (sometimes called Ecclesiasticus).

Yeshua's adaptation of the material in Sirach demonstrates that He was familiar with the wisdom literature of the rabbis. But that isn't the most important point about this use of rabbinic material. The crucial point is the *difference* Yeshua introduces. In both Sirach and Proverbs, Wisdom is personified, calling for men to come to "her" to receive instruction in living and the blessing of a righteous life. In both books, the narrator acts as the intermediary between Wisdom and the reader. But Yeshua changes all that. He is not the go-between. He is Wisdom itself. In other words, Yeshua does not cast Himself as the prophet or teacher pointing toward Wisdom (the divine instruction). He casts Himself in the role of Wisdom, and thereby claims that He *is* divine.

No one in His audience could have missed the change or the claim. Even if the audience didn't specifically recall the Sirach passage, everyone would have known the text of Proverbs. Yeshua's proclamation was unmistakable. No rabbi would ever make such a claim, at least no rabbi who did not believe that he was the manifestation of God Himself. The first point Yeshua makes is that *He* is the authority on Wisdom and that *He* is the only intermediary between God and men. Now that we see how powerful this verse really is, we also need to ask why Yeshua employed the imagery of the yoke.

The Hebrew concept of a yoke is almost always negative. Jews viewed yokes as a symbol of oppression. They had a long history of yoked captivity and tyranny. To suggest that people *willingly* take a yoke upon themselves would be inconceivable, except in one instance. The rabbis taught that voluntarily accepting the yoke of Torah was an experience of *freedom*, not of slavery and servitude. This positive use of *'ol* (Hebrew "yoke") is found in the *Ethics of the Fathers*: "Rabbi Nechunya ben Hakanah said: Whoever takes upon himself the yoke of Torah, from him will be taken away the yoke of government and the yoke of worldly care; but whoever throws off the yoke of Torah, upon him will be laid the yoke of government and the yoke of worldly care" (*Pirkei Avot* 3:6).

Add this background to our familiarity with the Matthew text. Yeshua declares His divine authority with regard to instructions for living. He is the *only* mediator of truth. Then He tells us to willingly accept His yoke, the yoke of kindness. What is that yoke? The only positive reference found in His own cultural setting claims that the yoke is Torah. Yeshua builds on the popular and familiar teaching of the rabbis and takes it one step further. Once again, He calls His followers to return to the only teaching that relieves us of the world of slavery – to return to His Torah since He is its divine author.

Perhaps this day should be remembered as a day when we acknowledge that Yeshua comes with supreme authority to bring us out of slavery by returning us to God's eternal instruction. Perhaps when the angels sang, "Peace on earth and good will toward men," they were offering in song what Yeshua offered in teaching. "Return unto me. Come back to My direction and be freed from worldly care."

(Sirach, the writings of Ben Sira, is part of the wisdom literature of the 2nd Century BC. You can read the text at this web site: http://st-takla.org/pub_Deuterocanon/Deuterocanon-Apocrypha_El-Asfar_El-Kanoneya_El-Tanya_5-Wisdon-of-Joshua-Son-of-Sirach.html)

17.

"And you, lie down on your left side, and lay the iniquity of the house of Israel on it. The number of the days that you shall lie down on it, you shall bear their iniquity." Ezekiel 4:4 (translation: A. Heschel)

Prophetic Calling

Bear – Who will respond to the call of the Lord? "Here I am," said Samuel. "Send me," said Isaiah. "It is accomplished," said Yeshua. But few and far between are the people who willingly take up God's call. Why? Perhaps the instructions to Ezekiel give us the answer. To be called by God is to bear the iniquity of others.

Ah, you thought that Yeshua bore it all. You thought that you were relieved from the duty of carrying the sins of others because He died as the perfect sacrifice. Think again. We encountered this Hebrew verb (*nasa*) in Isaiah 53:4. The Suffering Servant bears the sins of the people. So do the prophets. Certainly this cannot mean that Ezekiel is charged with the guilt of Israel and Judah. It means that Ezekiel is a substitute for the punishment that Israel and Judah deserve. The same is true of Yeshua. He bore our punishment. That had forensic value in God's moral government, but the act of sacrifice was an act of substitution, not forgiveness. Called to suffer, that's the role of those who would follow the Master. Called to suffer without cause for those who deserve to suffer. Do you still want to answer God's calling?

We might be willing to accept punishment for our own mistakes and disobedience. Accountability is a big word in Christian vocabulary today. But accountability is justifiable retribution. Personal excuses to the contrary, everyone understands the necessity and importance of personal judgment and discipline. But Christian vocabulary includes a word that defies human logic. That word is *nasa* – to bear. It is humanly inconceivable that I should bear the punishment others deserve. No legal system in this world condemns the innocent in place of the guilty. No system except God's system. To be called is to be called to substitutionary suffering. To forgive is to bear the guilt of the guilty, to willingly accept what should never be ours in order to remove the penalty from others. Prophets are not called to proclaim. They are called to stand in for God. They are called to display His suffering, to die for those who would rather live without the Father. Practical redemption is the choice to let God afflict me rather than bring His wrath to bear on those who most certainly merit it. Do you still want to answer God's calling?

What joy we experience when we take on the mantle of God's own grace! What victory we have when we act as His true stewards of men! And what honor we receive when we are shamed for His sake! The reason the world cannot understand or abide God's called-out ones is simple: they do not follow any form of common sense justice. They exhibit something the world cannot comprehend – the crucified God. Do you want to answer His calling? Good! He has counted you worthy to suffer in His name.

18.

*The law of the LORD is **perfect**, restoring the soul; the testimony of the LORD is sure, making wise the simple.* Psalm 19:7

Hebrew Perfection

Perfect – What is perfect? We usually think of perfection in mathematical terms. So perfect means without error. 100% correct. No mistakes. This Greek orientation leads to dilemmas for verses like Matthew 5:48. We can understand how God can be perfect, but how can God expect me to be without error or mistakes? It seems impossible.

We need to start over. The Hebrew concept of perfect is not the same as the mathematically-based Greek view. Here the word is *tamiym*. It means "blameless or complete." Over half of its occurrences in Scripture describe an animal used in sacrifice. Let me assure you that there is no animal on earth that is without error. The category of correctness doesn't apply to animals. To be perfect for a sacrifice, the animal needs only to be without spot or blemish. This standard is a *moral* one, not a cognitive one. I might get every answer on the algebra test wrong and God would still count me "perfect," as long as I am in alignment with His instructions. Conversely, I might be the smartest, most correct person on earth (do I hear the name "Solomon" in the background?) and still be hopelessly imperfect in God's eyes because I reject, ignore or disobey His Torah.

What is perfect? The psalmist gives us the bedrock picture of perfection – God's Torah. He employs both meanings of *tamiym* in this statement. First, God's Torah is morally blameless. There is nothing in His Torah that leads to sin or to ungodly actions, in front of Him or in front of other men. Living according to Torah is the epitome of *shalom* – peace with God and peacefulness among men. Secondly, God's Torah is complete. Everything I need to know about what really matters in life is in Torah. Of course, that doesn't mean Torah tells me how to balance my checkbook or find the quickest route to work or dozens of other trivial or not so trivial tasks in living. But from a Hebraic perspective, Torah tells me everything that really matters – and what matters most of all is that my life is pleasing to God. Think about that. If my life is pleasing to God, does anything else really make a very big difference? If my life is pleasing to God and God is sovereign over all life, don't you think He will take care of me? Yeshua had something to say about birds that applies to this kind of dependence.

The consonant root of *tamiym* is *Tau-Mem-Mem*. Its derivatives are translated "integrity," "complete," "perfect" and "entirely." It implies soundness, full health, what is completely truthful and what is ethically upright and undefiled. Notice these ideas are found in *activities*. What is truthful meets God's standards in speech. What is upright meets His standards in behavior and thought. What is pure meets His standards in ritual. Torah is the complete edition of God's standard, not the abridged handy pocket guide for successful living. That's why the study of Torah is one of the three most important spiritual disciplines of Judaism. Of course, the purpose of studying Torah is not the collection of information. It is the restoration of the "soul," as we shall see.

19.

*And He said, "Take your son, your favored one, Isaac, whom you love, and **go** to the land of Moriah, and offer him there as a burnt offering on one of the heights that I will point out to you."* Genesis 22:2 (JPS commentary on Genesis)

Picture Frames

Go – The test of Abraham concludes the journey of faith that began when God called Abram out of Ur. The text deliberately sets the frame of this journey with a repetition of the Hebrew phrase *lekh lakha* (go forth). This phrase occurs only *two* times in Scripture, at the beginning of the story of Abram and at the last test of Abraham. With this deliberate linguistic technique, the writer encapsulates the life of Abraham. We are meant to see these markers and reflect on Abraham's journey.

Abraham has already lost one son. Now it appears that he will lose the other. When God called Abram from Ur, he had to leave behind his family, his city and his culture. Abram became a wanderer for God, led only by divine intervention and guidance. Abraham was schooled in the discipline of dependence for nearly 100 years. During that time, we see Abraham's failures and triumphs. Now, at the end of the saga, Abraham is faced with the last, and perhaps the most difficult test. God asks (He does not demand) Abraham to voluntarily give up his beloved son (here is a typology of what will come thousands of years later) as a test of devotion and loyalty. To truly understand the magnitude of this request, we must enter into the story of Abram-Abraham. We must become this man, stripped of his past, a stranger to his surroundings, seeking to please a God who only occasionally speaks with him. We must read into the lines of the text the panoramic colors of his emotional struggles, his doubts, his collapsed marriage, his angst over his two sons. Imagine his faith walk. Strip yourself of the Scriptures. Tear yourself away from everything familiar. Break loose of your community. Follow only the voice of the Lord. After all that, are we prepared to burn to ashes the last earthly treasure we have?

This great story of faith (the Akedah – binding) is the hallmark of true discipleship. Until we stand with Abraham at the altar, looking down upon what we love most dearly, slaughtering knife in hand, we are not ready. We will fail this test. Perhaps that's why God waited 100 years to put it to Abraham. Perhaps that's why God asked but did not command. Perhaps that's why God framed this story as the final step of Abraham's journey. God knows when we are ready. Quite often we don't have any clue. We live day to day as if our gradual and incremental progression toward faithfulness is all we can muster. Then God comes with a body-blow. "Take your son, your only son, the one you love, and go forth."

Abraham learned the appropriate response, *hinneni* ("here I am, Master"), over the course of a lifetime. That is the way God teaches all His children. A long obedience in the same direction (as Eugene Peterson rightly noted). God began a frame around your life the day you heard His first call. Now you and I are watching for the other edge of the frame so that we can also say, "Here I am, my Lord. What would You have me do?"

20.

*And you shall love YHWH your Elohim with **all your heart** and with all your* nephesh *and with all your might* Deuteronomy 6:5 (my adjusted translation)

A Little Deeper

All your heart – *be-kol levavha*. Try saying it. "With all your heart." YHWH wants – and expects – your whole heart commitment to Him. How will I know that I have made that commitment? I will follow His instructions for living in His world. This second verse in the Shema recognizes the obligation and the honor God has given me. I fulfill His *mitzvot* because each one is a way for me to demonstrate how much I love Him. There is no legalism here, only joy. "Lord, I love to do Your will."

But what happens when I don't fulfill His instructions? What happens when I succumb to the inner rebellion that pushes me away from a disciplined life of joyful observance? What happens when I obey out of compulsion or legalism rather than gratitude? Does this commandment change depending on my spiritual condition?

No. Not at all. To love God with all my heart is to love Him with both my positive and negative propensities.

The rabbis taught that *be-kol levavha* means that I am to love God with both human inclinations, the inclination to good (*yetzer ha-tov*) and the inclination to evil (*yetzer ha-ra*). "It is incumbent on man to bless YHWH for the evil in the same way as for the good." Why would the rabbis teach such a thing? They noticed that there is a redundant *bet* in the word *levavha*. The word heart is *lev*, spelled in Hebrew *lamed-bet*, but in this verse, the word is spelled *lamed-bet-bet* before the pronoun "your" (*kaf*) is added. Why the double *bet*? The rabbis taught that the double *bet* represented one *bet* for each of the two inclinations. Therefore, *both* inclinations are included in the command to love God.

Consider the psychological impact of this teaching. In our usual religious thinking, men are bent toward evil. Some theological doctrines even suggest that men are *inherently* evil, born as sinners. In other words, it is not simply the case that men sin. It is rather that men *cannot do anything except sin* until they are granted a new constitution by God's grace. They cannot love the Lord with all their hearts because their hearts are entirely wicked. Even their good deeds bear no positive moral currency. But if I view men as the locus of a battlefield between the two inclinations, then good deeds have positive moral value no matter what struggle is raging within me. Good deeds won't save me because I am still accountable for my bad deeds, but there is a reason to continue to perform good deeds in spite of my sins. Good deeds please God and bless His creation. When I follow His instructions, I feed the good inclination. When I don't follow His instructions, I feed the evil inclination – but even in my failure I am still called to love Him. Out of my sins, I am still exhorted to change direction – to start again and make it right. From the Jewish perspective there is absolutely no situation in life that does not demand honoring God. I can never throw up my hands and say, "Well, I'm just a sinner," because there are two *vav's* in *levavha*.

How often do we become discouraged in our walk because we fall down? The *yitzer ha-ra* wins one round of the match, or two, and we think, "I'll never be able to love God with all my heart. My heart is a mess. I am always struggling. I'm not pure in my affection for the Lord. I'm a loser!" At that moment we need a rabbi to say, "You may love the Lord our God with your *yetzer ha'ra* and your *yetzer ha-tov*. Why are you so downcast? If you do what is right, won't it be acceptable? Let the anguish of your *yitzer ha-ra* become the source of blessing HaShem."

What change would happen to you if you realized you are the *battlefield*, not the combatant?

21.

It is a trustworthy statement; if any man aspires to the office of **overseer**, *it is a fine work he desires to do.* 1 Timothy 3:1 NASB

The Boss-man?

Overseer – But what about Carol or Ann or Linda or Miriam? What if they desire to be "overseers"? Ah, if only Paul weren't so gender conscious. But wait a minute! If we look at the Greek text, we find that the verse doesn't say, "if any *man*." It says, "if *anyone*." The reason the NASB and other translations introduce gender specificity is a result of the *next* verse with its statement about "the husband of one wife." The *assumption* is that this must be about men since the prohibition only applies to men. But not so fast!

Let's start with the theme. That theme is *service*, not authority. Sometimes translated "bishop," the word *episkopos* literally means "a watchman, someone who looks after something." Because this term was used in classical Greek for officials who were sent to outlying provinces, we have assumed that the word is about an *office* (notice the NASB translation), not a role played by anyone in the Body. But what do we find when we look for the word *episkopos* in the LXX? We find words associated with visiting (like *paqad*). Sometimes the subject is God Himself. Sometimes it is men. But there is little to suggest that these "visitors" are rulers or officials simply because they have been sent. Since Paul is speaking in general about the theme of providing *service to others*, I suspect that his view of an "overseer" has more to do with hands-on help than it has to do with micromanagement. And I doubt very much that these people came with titles in front of their names.

How does one become an *episkopos*? Perhaps by desiring to help. Perhaps by being where the work needs to be done. Perhaps by offering to direct the project or the effort. Perhaps by making sure that *everything anyone else needs is provided*. One thing is abundantly clear. Being an *episkopos* has nothing to do with getting the credit.

Now what about Carol? Why can't a woman be an *episkopos*? Don't women desire to be helpful visitors? Aren't women capable of directing endeavors of the Body? Of course they are. In fact, there are many examples in both the Old and New Testaments of women who were overseers in every sense of the word except the Church-endorsed "title" (which came much later). The entire exclusion of women from the role of director for helping depends on Paul's subsequent statement, "the husband of one wife." But that is a completely culturally-dependent condition. It is the prohibition against polygamy, still practiced by the wealthy in the first century. It is not about divorce. It is about the inevitable stress caused by more than one wife at the same time. Why doesn't Paul make a statement about the monogamy of women? Because there was absolutely no need to. Polyandry was not practiced in the first century Mediterranean world.

The conditions for being an overseer are limited to these: purity, goodness, temperance, modesty, not greedy, not argumentative, gentle, not prideful and not a novice. Gender has nothing to do with it. Living by the Spirit has everything to do with it. Those translations that suggest this is an office limited only to men are more a reflection of the male hierarchy's desire for power than they are a reflection of the nature of God.

144

22.

*You foolish Galatians, who has **bewitched** you, before whose eyes Jesus Christ was publicly portrayed as crucified?* Galatians 3:1 NASB

Twenty Centuries Later

Bewitched – Have we been fooled? Would Paul say the same thing to us if he showed up at our doorsteps? "You *undisciplined Christians*, who has *cast an evil eye upon* you?" Perhaps that translation reveals a bit more in this text. We are prone to think of "foolish" as if it were simply a matter of lack of intelligence, but we must remember that Paul is Jewish and in Jewish thought, mental mistakes have moral consequences. This word (*anoetos*) implies that a lack of intelligence is exhibited in a lack of control over lusts. The Galatians (and others) didn't simply lack knowledge. They lacked discipline.

Paul wants to know how this happened. His question reveals two underlying elements. The question itself suggests that they *should have been disciplined*. Right understanding should lead to right living. The fact that the Galatians are not living according to expectation is a clear indication that their theology is also a mess. How we behave is *not* divorced from our apprehension of reality. People *do* what they really value regardless of the words they say or the statements of faith they proclaim. These people aren't *carnal Christians* (do some research and discover who really invented that term). They are sinners in need of repentance. The second implication of this question arises from the use of the Greek word *baskaino*. The word means "to cast an evil eye." It is a word about *superstition*.

It describes people who believe in magic, sorcery and legend. In other words, *baskaino* is a word about people who *don't trust the sovereignty of God*. What Paul suggests with this word is that these Galatians are *still pagan* in their thoughts and practices. That's why they are *foolish* and *bewitched*. They haven't come to grips with the truth about Yeshua HaMashiach. How does Paul know that they are still thinking and acting like pagans? He looks at their behavior! What does he see? He sees people who are not living according to Torah. You can check out the list of foolish actions in Galatians 5:19-21. Where does that list come from? Did Paul just make it up? No, each of those actions is a violation of Torah.

Christians generally accept Harnack's proposal that Judaism and Christianity parted company in the second century. This proposal implies that Christians don't need the life instructions found in the Torah since Christianity is not Jewish. But current scholarship has overturned Harnack's theory and seriously questions replacement theology. The historical record shows that believing communities practiced Torah living well into the 4th Century. In fact, it was a small group of intellectuals who eventually turned the Church away from its natural Jewish foundation. So, when Paul writes to the Galatians, he doesn't have to explain a new code of conduct to them. He knows, and they should have known, that Torah obedience is the standard. It is only their undisciplined thought and action that keeps them locked in pagan ways. I wonder if the Church today isn't a great deal more like those pagan Galatians than it is like the intended believing and practicing Body that Paul so desired. I suppose we will have to look and see, won't we?

Leadership
The "Help Wanted" Job

If you listen to the advertising, leadership is simply a matter of getting the right training, having the right attitude and applying the right techniques. Apparently, everyone can become a leader. In fact, if we accept the culture's view of leadership, everyone *must become* a leader. From education to business, from the church to politics, we need *leaders* (so we think). Of course, this begs the question, "If everyone is a leader, who will follow?"

The contemporary view of leadership suggests that leaders are models of visionary prognostication, motivational insight and personal charisma. We expect our leaders to demonstrate an uncanny ability to *control* circumstances. Perhaps that's why we tend to elect leaders with the proper *image* rather than a biblical morality. The leader's motto today is "I get things done." In too many cases, this is an excuse for "the ends justify the means." Today leaders are expected to have demonstrable success, personal and public power, plenty of trophy accomplishments and, above all, an observable sense of self-confidence. The world makes heroes and heroines of success models, usually attributing the title "leader" to anyone who lives the "good life." Since we are convinced that the world can be controlled with the proper amount of correctly applied effort, we look for those among us who appear to be in control of everything around them. Until they stumble, we treat them as demy-gods, proclaiming that this is what leadership really looks like.

Unfortunately, none of these features seem to matter when we examine the biblical idea of leadership. In fact, from the biblical perspective, it would be more appropriate to say that biblical leaders are prime examples of *reluctance*. Once we understand the true role of the biblical leader, we will readily agree. From a biblical perspective, no one actually wants this job. Those who do are to be feared since they are typically motivated by hubris rather than humility before God. The biblical leader realizes that he or she is called to suffering, rejection, misunderstanding, and even death. That's why the prophets begged God to choose someone else, why Moses claimed inadequacy, why David delayed and why the apostles never sought power or prestige. Even the Christ displayed reluctance overcome by obedience.

As we examine leadership from a biblical point of view, we will discover that character counts. Men and women whom God chooses *rarely* have sterling resumes, even after they have been employed. What we find are ordinary people called to extraordinary tasks; tasks that can only be accomplished through the Spirit. In stark opposition to the world's view, *not everyone can be a biblical leader.* Not everyone is called to be a biblical leader. And those who are called often wish they could opt out and simply attend classes in better communication.

Abraham Heschel's most telling insight comes from his remark about Job. In the biblical model, Job is the paradigm of a leader. He is a man of misfortune at the hand of God, a man of trouble, acquainted with grief, a man of worship in the face of unmitigated agony, a man who questions not only his own existence but the justice of God. Such a man demonstrates the character of biblical leadership because he is *called* to more than himself. As Heschel points out, "No Job arose in Hellas. Indeed, his outcry is part of the drama in which God and man are involved with one another."[28]

The Greek-based Western world cannot understand such a man as a leader. A model of moral integrity, perhaps, but a *leader*? No! Not for us! Job's story is a story of the over-

---

[28] Abraham Heschel, *A Passion for Truth*, p. 290.

overwhelming consciousness of God's sovereignty, not of a man's individual prowess. And for precisely this reason, Job could not have emerged from Hellas. Job is a man of Scripture, called by God to God's purposes. This is biblical leadership. And it doesn't come comfortably.

1.

But I do not allow a woman to teach, nor to **exercise authority** *over a man, but to be in silence.* 1 Timothy 2:12

Name Withheld

Exercise Authority – You have got to be kidding me! That is probably the immediate contemporary reaction to the face-value interpretation of Paul's remark. If what Paul says is really the biblical model for the proper actions of women, then a whole lot of us stand condemned on this one. Paul seems to be saying (and the Church seems to be endorsing) women are to shut up, be subservient and take care of the home. If this is really the biblical intention, then we sin when women are in authority, teach, direct, manage, preach or speak both *inside* and *outside* the Body. No wonder some women think Paul is a misogynist.

For more than a thousand years, the Church employed a Greek philosophical paradigm when it interpreted this verse. That Greek model comes directly from Plato and Aristotle who taught that women were *defective* men. It isn't too much of an exaggeration to say Greek philosophers despised women, considering them intellectually inferior, emotionally immature and generally incapable of the actions and attitudes of men. The early church fathers were immersed in Greek philosophy so it is not surprising to find their exegesis reflects Plato and the Academy. As a result of this paradigm, the Church and the culture engaged in withholding education, development and leadership from women. Predictably, the result merely confirmed what the paradigm taught: women were inferior.

But Paul is no Platonist. He is a Second Temple rabbi. His approach to the role and status of women is based in Scripture, not philosophy. A thorough analysis of Paul's full understanding of women would reveal exactly what he shares in Galatians 3:28. In the Body, there is no hierarchy! All the world's false distinctions – Jew and Gentile, slave and free, male and female – are overcome and set aside. So, what do we do with this apparent misogyny.

In the Greek text, Paul deliberately switches from the plural "women" when he talks about godly behavior for the whole congregation to the singular "woman" when he exhorts Timothy in this passage. In other words, Paul has *a particular woman* in mind, someone who is causing plenty of disturbance and distress among the Body. Paul directs *this* woman to be silent. Why? Because she is *usurping* authority, grasping at control that is not properly hers. The Greek verb here, *authentein*, is used only one time in all the New Testament and for good reason. It comes from the word *authentes* which means "a self-appointed killer with one's own hand." In other words, this verb is about *domination*, not leadership. It is associated with a murderer, an absolute dictator, a tyrant. Paul says this woman seeks to rule with an iron hand. Her actions must not be allowed because in the Body there is no place for an autocrat, whether man or woman. Telling her to be silent employs a Hebrew expression about serious contemplation of humility.

Paul, the apostle of unity in the Body, the messenger of equally distributed grace, the herald of the destruction of all class and gender distinctions, could not possibly instruct the Body to relegate one gender to the corner. This instruction is about an unruly, unrestrained person who wants to run the show. In this case, the subject is a women, but it could just as well have been a man. In the Body, this sort of action doesn't work.

Oh yes, and Paul is so concerned about the circumstances and the woman involved that he doesn't name her. Even in his discipline, he demonstrates consideration.

Now that you are no longer under the false, Greek-based misunderstanding of Paul's concern, don't you think it's time to correct twenty centuries of mistakes?

2.

*"But **not so with you**, but let him who is the greatest among you become as the youngest, and the leader as the servant."* Luke 22:26

Code of Honor

Not So With You – The leadership fad will run its course. Eventually we will learn that leadership is a verb, not a noun. Then we will realize ubiquitous leadership training is wasted effort. We should be training those who are born leaders, not expecting everyone born to become a leader through training. Once we see this distinction, we can concentrate on Yeshua's insight into leadership. Leadership is serving, a verb for everyone. It is the application of each person's unique gift for the benefit of others. Leading is serving someone else according to the way God made me.

Yeshua's disciples thought leadership was a matter of status. The greater the rank, the more important the person. Those who lead are at the top of the pyramid. But Yeshua turns it upside-down. Serving others is God's measure of leading. It's not a position. It's an action – an action that anyone can perform.

Now that we've settled this issue, we should notice one important implication. The phrase "not so with you" (in Greek *humeis ouk outos*) is gender neutral. Oh, it's clear

Yeshua is addressing His disciples, but we can hardly justify the claim that His statement applies *only* to them. Yeshua declares that anyone who is a disciple will follow this exhortation. So, every man and every woman who claims Yeshua as Lord will lead by serving another. Seems obvious, doesn't it? If it is so obvious, then how can we justify the claim that husbands are the rulers of their homes and wives are to be subservient to husbands' wishes? Should we ignore Yeshua's declaration? Does serving another apply to everything *except* marriage? Hardly! If a husband is a follower for Yeshua, then he leads by serving his wife, not by demanding she serve him. His leadership is exhibited in his willingness to give up his agenda and take care of hers. He lives for her. This, by the way, is exactly the behavioral expression of Yeshua's sacrifice for the Body. If leadership is service, then there is no room at all for status or ranked authority in the Christian home.

Most Christians are quick to apply the servant-leader vocabulary to circumstances outside their homes. They try to emulate Yeshua's behavior at work, at school, at church and in social settings among others. But when it comes to marriage, the principle is suddenly abandoned. Now men rule. Now the curse of Eve puts a wife under her husband's authority. Now the man is the "head" of the home by divine proclamation. Now women are to be silent, submissive and subservient. And we call this leadership? Who are we kidding?

Oh, yes, before all the women stop cheering, remember that the principle applies to both sexes.

3.

*The **children** of Amram were Aaron, Moses and Miriam.* 1 Chronicles 5:29

Starting Out Right

Children – It's true that the children of Amram were Aaron, Moses and Miriam, but this isn't what the Hebrew text says. The Hebrew word *oovnei* appears a second time in the same verse, but it isn't translated "and the children of." It's translated "and the sons of" because that's what *oovnei* means. So, if the verse literally says, "And the sons of Amram were," then why do we change it to "children"? Ah, you say. It's obvious. Miriam is not a son. She is a daughter. You're right, of course, but by changing the translation "and the sons" to "and the children" reveals our implicit chauvinism. You see, the Hebrew text isn't mistaken. Miriam has the same status as the sons, Moses and Aaron. *oovnei* might be an idiomatic way of saying "children," but one can hardly overlook the fact that it is primarily about males.

Think about Miriam. She is a priestess. She is a central figure in the story of the Exodus. Her actions are responsible for saving Moses. She is a prophet. In fact, she is the second person to be designated a prophet at this point in the Torah. Micah 6:4 tells us that she was divinely commissioned as a leader. Tell that to the theologians who proclaim that women are not to lead men. Who's right? MacArthur, Piper and Grudem or God? Miriam's death is prominently mentioned in Scripture while nearly everyone else in the Exodus account fades into the background. Finally, there's this verse. In a chapter about male genealogies, we find Miriam's name. Scripture doesn't make mistakes. We do. We have ignored the place God gives this woman because we read our mistaken misogynic theology into the Bible. It's time to get started on the right foot. It's time to pay careful attention to what the text says, not what we want it to say.

Hebrews 13:6 quotes Psalm 118:6. "The Lord is my helper, I will not be afraid. What shall man do to me?" We acknowledge that God is our *'ezer*. Because He cares for us, protects us and provides for us, we do not need to fear any man. But this special word, *'ezer*, is the same word God uses to designate the role of the wife, the *'ezer kenegdo*. When my wife exhibits the full design God built into her, I am cared for, protected and provided for. My wife follows in the footsteps of Miriam, an *'ezer* among her people. She was God's chosen instrument of proclamation, leadership, comfort and compassion. If you want a role model as a woman, you might start with Miriam.

Our misguided theology usually highlights the times when Miriam stumbled. Ah, she's human, just like the rest of us. Did Aaron stumble? Did Moses? Apparently God loves to use those who stumble. Did you think that being a leader meant being perfect? As far as I can tell, every biblical leader trips along the way (with one notable exception, of course). What makes us think that failure disqualifies anyone from God's use? So, we have a new beginning today. We see Miriam in a new light. Maybe that will spur us to see God's women differently, and stop getting in the way of what He is doing with His chosen servants (plural, female noun).

5.

*Yet I will **exult** in the LORD, I will rejoice in the God of my salvation.* Habakkuk 3:18

End of Days

Exult – Better read the context before you start the celebration. Habakkuk has just recounted the circumstances of disaster. The trees do not bear fruit. The vines fail. The fields have no crops. The flocks are scattered. Now that total economic collapse is at hand, *exult* in the Lord. The Hebrew verb *'alaz* means "to rejoice, to be jubilant." It is party-time. This kind of celebration is a full endorsement of the message. God Himself exults over Israel. But here the prophet finds a way to exult in the worst of times. When everything seems to be at the end of days, there is still a reason to exult. God is our salvation.

Of course, that does not mean that we will escape. His salvation does not mean that suddenly all will be turned to the good. It doesn't mean a short trip to the heavenly gates. It means confident trust in God's ways, even if those ways mean I will die. The righteousness man is knocked down seven times. That's an idiom for being killed. Yet he rejoices. He will rise again. The righteousness man can say, "Even if You slay me, yet I will worship You." "Even if He does not rescue us from your fiery furnace, we will not bow down or serve this idol." "Even if this cup cannot pass from me, yet Your will be done." The message is the same throughout Scripture. Circumstances are *not* the measure of God's goodness. I trust who He is, not what He does. I celebrate Him. The situation is only a distraction.

Perhaps we can relate to the economic woes of the prophet. Perhaps we need to bring his insight into our contemporary culture. There is a lot of bad news on the horizon. There are a lot of economic woes. There is more risk today than most of us have faced in a lifetime. Circumstances tend to diminish our hope. If we pay attention to our troubles, we are likely to miss the biblical perspective. "The question of man's position before God is *the* question of existence. Everything else depends on it."[29] The answer depends on our understanding of the character of our Father. It does not depend on His plans, choices, designs or purposes.

---

[29] Wurthwein, *TDNT, Vol. IV*, p. 985.

If the Hebrew idea of faith is trustworthiness, then faith is placing my life in the hands of the one who is ultimately trustworthy. I have seen His faithfulness in history. I will see it again when I look back over my life a thousand years from now. But today, I celebrate. I exult in the God who rescues – and I trust that He will once more.

6.

If it is the anointed priest who has incurred guilt, so that **blame** *falls upon the people, . . .* Leviticus 4:3

Reluctant Leaders

Blame – The principle characteristic of a *biblical* leader is reluctance. Men and women marked by God for leadership roles almost always wish they were not chosen. When you meet people who desire to lead, you would be wise to run the other way. Those who want the job are more than likely to let ego and pride determine their choices. When that happens, the people suffer – sometimes greatly. No one can truly lead without the Lord and those who lead with Him are constantly reminded of their insufficiency. Watch out for the ones who think they can handle the job! Anyone who wants to *make* history will probably break the people doing so.

In this passage in Leviticus, we see one of the reasons why leadership is so terrifying. If the high priest (the anointed priest) accidentally or unintentionally sins, there is a direct consequence to the people. Read that again. When the leader falls, even unintentionally, *all* the assembly bears the consequences. We see this principle played out over and over in Scripture. The sin of one affects many. Sha'ul builds an entire theology on this connection. But somehow we don't think it applies to us today. Oh, we are quite happy to cite the connection with David's sins or recall the passage in Romans 5. But apparently we believe that God set aside this principle of the universe when Yeshua died on the cross. Or maybe we are so dull in our discernment that we don't see what's happening until it's too late. But the principle remains true. Leadership bears enormous responsibility. A leader who displeases the Lord will cause great harm to all who follow him. His actions, even his accidental offenses, can bring 'ashmah (guilt) upon the people. It follows that no man or woman can hope to lead unless they have lives of intense obedience and continuous examination. Even the smallest error can bring wrath. Who would want to carry such a burden?

Of course, God does call men and women to these roles. They may resist, as Moses clearly demonstrates, but God knows the hearts of His leaders and He is willing to take the risk. That is all the more reason why leadership should be treated with the greatest of care. God *trusts* those He calls to lead. To fail in the task is not simply to cause guilt to fall on the people. It is also to violate God's trust. There is a good reason why Moses is described as the most humble man who walked the earth. He knew he wasn't up to the challenge.

Today leadership is often seen as a prize to be gained. Today we hold up celebrity leaders as if they were a little less than Mount Olympus gods. Today we think that everyone should become a leader. We live among a generation of incalculable hubris. And we will undoubtedly pay the price for such folly. Payment is written into the fabric of the universe. Our leaders *crave* leadership. "In that day, flee to the hills" would be an appropriate warning. No man can serve two masters. The hubris of leadership certainly stands opposed to the way of the Lord.

Do you desire to be called "Boss," "Chief," "Chairman," or "President"? Do you realize what you are asking to bear? Are you reluctant, or are you anxious to rise to the top? Perhaps a good dose of Leviticus will bring you to your senses.

7.

*But He answered and said "When it is evening, you say, 'It will be fair weather, for the sky is **red**.'"* Matthew 16:2

Folk Lore

Red – "Red sky in the morning, sailors take warning." Yes, centuries after Yeshua mentioned this already common bit of folk lore, we still use the same expression. Of course, Yeshua's point is that we are quite capable of applying folk lore prophecies about the weather, which everyone knows is as unpredictable as anything on earth, and yet we seem incapable of applying the clear signs of God, which are undoubtedly the most stable things on earth.

With that in mind, perhaps we would do well to recall some of those sayings that help us measure the spiritual weather.

"It is a bad thing to be satisfied spiritually. . . . Our reach must exceed our grasp. If we have only what we have experienced, we have nothing; . . ." Oswald Chambers

"The hallmark of an authentic evangelicalism is not the uncritical repetition of old traditions but the willingness to submit every tradition, however ancient, to fresh biblical scrutiny and, if necessary, reform." John Stott

"One thing is clear to me: the temptation of power is greatest when intimacy is a threat. Much Christian leadership is exercised by people who do not know how to develop healthy, intimate relationships and have opted for power and control instead. Many Christian empire-builders have been people unable to give and receive love..." Henri Nouwen

"Maybe they'd be O.K. if somewhere along the way they'd had true friends, defined as a group of people who share a mutual inability to take each other seriously. Maybe they'd be prepared for what is about to happen if they'd subordinated their quest for immortality to the joys of domestic ridicule." David Brooks

"Do not think that love, in order to be genuine, has to be extraordinary. What we need is to love without getting tired." Mother Teresa

"People seek methods of learning to know God. Is it not much shorter and more direct to simply do everything for the love of Him? There is no finesse about it. One only has to do it generously and simply." Brother Lawrence

"The Church's mission is not to accommodate her language to the existing language, to disguise herself so as to slip in unnoticed and blend in with the existing culture. Her mission is to confront the language of the existing culture with a language of her own." Peter Leithart

8.

"Give, and good measure will be given to you, pressed down and shaken together, and running over, they will pour into your lap. For what ever measure you deal out to others, it will be dealt to you in return." Luke 6:38

Life or Death

Give - There are two Greek verbs that mean "to give." *Doreomai* means "to give" in the sense of "to grant." With this verb, the emphasis falls on the giver and his generosity. This verb is related to *dorea* (gift) and is used of God's supernatural gift, freely given because of His character. But in this verse, the Greek verb is *didomi*. The emphasis of *didomi* is not on the giver but on the gift itself. The noun, *doron,* is used for offering to God where the emphasis is not on the one making the offering but rather on the actual offering made. Now we can apply this insight to Yeshua's statement. We discover that Yeshua is *not* emphasizing *us*. He is not commending our worthy effort. His emphasis in the Greek text is on the gift, *not* the giver. He is not congratulating us on our generosity or noble character. Instead, he is pointing toward *what we give*. Why?

I suspect that most of us would rather read this verse as if it were a personal commendation about our worthiness. It isn't! It isn't an acknowledgement of how wonderful we are because giving *was the expected norm* in the close communities of Israel. There was no welfare, no entitlements, no social security, no government agencies to look after those in need. If anything were to be done, it had to be done by other members of the community. And it was done! It was *expected* that anyone who was able to help would do so. In fact, those who did not *voluntarily* assist were consider greedy, even if they had only two cents. Why? Because greed was the display of the *unwillingness* to offer assistance whenever one was able to do so. Greed was characterized by placing myself ahead of the needs of others. And in the communal society of Israel, greed killed!

In order to understand why giving and greed are polar opposites, we must make a radical paradigm shift. The basic tenet of modern capitalism is the assumption that the available resources of the world are not limited. Yes, we all know that there is only a finite amount of everything, but the economic engine that runs the capitalist society operates *as if* there are no *practical* limits. In other words, we really don't think we will run out of stuff anytime soon. But this is not true in the Semitic, Middle-Eastern cultures. Those cultures have a very strong paradigm about the *limited* amount of resources. If everything is truly limited *right now*, then life is a Zero-Sum game. There is only so much of the pie, so the more that I accumulate, the less there is for others. In this worldview, greed kills because greed means that I take more than I need and ignore the fact that my possession limits the available resources for others.

We have a hard time thinking of the world's resources as strictly limited. These days we don't operate in the Zero-Sum world. We think in terms of making *more*, not in terms of depriving others. But in Yeshua's world, lack of generosity meant someone died. So, giving was absolutely expected. If I took more of the pie, you had less. If I took too much, you had none. Therefore, *what* I give is vital to the well-being of the community. I must give any amount that exceeds what I need (not what I want).

Let this paradigm shift sink in for awhile – and then we will look at "Give" once more.

9.

*YHWH enters into judgment with the elders and princes of His people' "It is you who have devoured the vineyard; the plunder of the poor is in your houses. What do you mean by crushing My people and **grinding** the face of the poor?"* Isaiah 3:14-15

God's Social Justice

Grinding – "So the common man has been humbled and the man of importance has been abased, but do not forgive them" (Isaiah 2:9). What? Isaiah prays that God *not* forgive.

What insensitive, irreligious attitude is this? Can you imagine any preacher rising in the pulpit and beseeching God *not to forgive* those who listen from the pews? No wonder the people murdered the prophets. No one wants to hear a man of God proclaim that his sins will go unremitted. But Isaiah had good reason for such a shocking prayer. Both the common man and powerful leader were abusing the poor. They were *grinding* the face of God's most precious ones in order to fill their houses with luxury.

The Hebrew verb, *tacan*, means "to crush, to grind into small pieces (as in a mill)." The idiomatic expression, "to grind the face of the poor," means to oppress the poor, to use them for one's own advantage. If there were ever a word that describes the economic disparity in this world, this is that word. Remember it. *Tacan* (tä·khan'). When you pay $5.00 for your next cup of Starbuck's, think of *tacan*, and the $2 a day that the harvester gets paid to gather those beans. When you try on those khakis at the Gap store, think of *tacan* and the 15 cents that the single mother was paid to sew them at the factory in Honduras. Spend $30 on a Maidenform bra. She was paid 18 cents to make it. Enjoy the "Kelly Reed" dresses at major discount stores. Someone breathing polluted air and living in squalor outside Port-au-Prince worked for $0.12 per hour to make them. How about that pair of Nike shoes? The company contributed $2 a day to the worker who produced 12 pairs. *Tacan*. Isaiah applies the word to the *common* man as well as the community leadership. How will we survive his declaration, "Do not forgive them!"?

I have a dream. My dream is not as powerful or as noble or as far-reaching as the dream of Dr. Martin Luther King. It is a simple dream. It is a dream about a village in Honduras. The village doesn't need a name. There are dozens of them. Any one will do. It is home to fifty people, mostly women and children. The men are gone to look for work or simply escape. The children eat when they can, once a day if they are lucky. There are no sewers, no clean water, no electricity, no medical clinics, no schools. In twenty-five years, most of these people will be dead. My dream is not for them. My dream is for those who will be born between now and the time this village falls into ruin. My dream is to turn this village into a community, a group of people who are productive, who care about each other because they aren't desperate about living, who have discovered there is someone from the bubble-world of Nike shoes and Starbuck's and Maidenform who will sacrifice for them, not to give them relief but to give them dignity. As I said, it is a simple dream. But my feet seem to take me there whenever they can.

10.

*She **did not** listen to the voice; she **did not** take correction; she **did not** trust in YHWH; she **did not** draw near to her God.* Zephaniah 3:2

The Pursuit of Power (1)

Did Not – Zephaniah speaks out against the oppressing city. His words are harsh, convicting, condemning. They are less a call to repentance than they are a proclamation of judgment. "Woe to her rebelling and being defiled," says the prophet. Perhaps we need to hear his words afresh. Everything he says about the ancient society is true of our civilization, one hundred times over.

In this verse, Zephaniah provides four accusations, each one beginning with the Hebrew word *lo*. This is one of two Hebrew words meaning no or not. It is used to express the *unconditional prohibitions* of the commandments ("You shall not"). In Zephaniah's mouth, this word strikes the hammer

165

blows of impending doom. "You never listened; you never took correction; you never trusted in YHWH; you never drew near." Now it is too late. Just as God instructs Jeremiah not to pray for His people, not to delay their chastisement, so God's word through Zephaniah is the flash of lightning before the inevitable thunder. Judgment is coming and nothing will stop it.

What did this oppressing city do to deserve such terrible consequences? Nothing more than we find in our own land. *Lo shamah.* You did not listen-obey. God's instructions were clearly given. Every person heard them and agreed to follow them throughout the generations. There is no excuse. Today we look out upon the land and see very, very few who uphold Torah. Certainly the culture is adamantly opposed, fighting even the smallest remnant of Torah suggestions. We did not listen.

Lo laqha. We did not grasp; we did not seize; we did not take on the correction of the Lord. He provided it time and again. He reminded, cajoled, encouraged, remonstrated and engineered circumstances to bring us to our senses. But we refused. At every crossroad of opportunity, we chose power rather than humility, pride rather than repentance. We did not take.

Lo vataha. We did not trust. *Batah* is a verb expressing confidence, reliance and security. It is the *defining* action of those who truly follow Him. It is the replacement of retirement accounts, bank balances, insurance, security alarms, body guards, job guarantees and anything else that becomes the foundation of our perceived security. In a world demon-possessed by fears of the future, God offers safety. But we preferred money. We did not trust.

Lo kareva. We did not draw near. There is a procedure for drawing near, a ritual that brings us close to Him. We have ignored it and created our own approach. So we pray, "Lord, be present in the place today." But why should He? We approach without purity. We require Him to join us instead of coming to His house His way. Across the land we act as if God draws near at *our* invitation while we summarily dismiss His. We did not draw near.

And what is the result? The oppressing city will be destroyed. God will start over with the remnant.

Zephaniah's proclamation is the sound of the hammer about to flatten the metal on the anvil. When the hammer strikes its blow, none will escape. The righteous and the wicked will perish together while God reshapes the earth. Their ultimate destinies may be different, but collateral damage is the consequence of living in a civilization of "did not."

Today is a great day to be alive. We who know Him have much to do before He arrives. There are many, so many, who need rescue. There are many who need the favor of righteous acts. There is light to be shed abroad. Before judgment, there is re-collection. Who will you rescue from the "did not" society today?

11.

*Her princes inside her are **roaring lions**; her judges are **evening wolves**...* Zephaniah 3:3

The Pursuit of Power (2)

Roaring Lions/Evening Wolves - "The hunger of the powerful knows no satiety; the appetite grows on what it feeds. Power exalts itself and is incapable of yielding to any transcendent judgment; . . . It is the bitter irony of history that the common people, who are devoid of power and are the prospective victims of its abuse, are the first to become the ally of him who accumulated power. Power is spectacular, while its end, the moral law, is inconspicuous."[30]

"A democracy cannot exist as a permanent form of government. It can only exist until the voters discover that they can vote themselves largesse (generous gifts) from the public treasury. From that moment on, the majority always votes for the candidates promising the most benefits from the public treasury, with the result that a democracy always collapses over loose fiscal policy, [which is] always followed by a dictatorship."[31]

When Thomas Jefferson said that public debt was the greatest enemy of democracy, he was undoubtedly reflecting on the indisputable historical record of past civilizations. From Egypt to Rome, from Greece to the Holy Roman Empire, power corrupted every hierarchy of leadership, eventually resulting in massive spending at the expense of those who produced. No civilization has ever recovered from the addiction of the powerful.

But Jefferson need not have looked further than his Bible. In fact, all he had to do was read the prophet Zephaniah. The Bible makes it abundantly clear that peace and prosperity are the result of *righteousness*, not power. Zephaniah warned us all. Power breeds lions and wolves; lions whose roar is the sound of mayhem and slaughter, wolves whose feasting on the vulnerable leaves nothing for the morning. Woe to any people who believe that the powerful will save them. Woe to those who, given power, oppress the helpless. Of all the world's addictions, power is to be feared the most

---

[30] Abraham Heschel, *The Prophets*, Vol. 1, p. 159-160.

[31] Alexander Tyler, *The Fall of the Athenian Republic*

for it is the unbridled warrant for destruction. No man or woman who *wishes* to be powerful is fit to wield its sword. This is why God chooses leaders who are unsuited for the task. This is why God is the only King, the final authority and the arbiter of the good. No man can hold the sword of power for long without abusing its force and any man who thinks he is able to do so without the humility that comes from standing before a Holy God is a bigger fool than the Father of Lies.

What is the biblical solution to the addiction of power? Prayer! A leader who is not in constant conversation with the Father is a ravenous beast in civil disguise. Prayer makes us human. The lack of prayer turns us into roaring lions and evening wolves. The only antidote to power is standing in His presence – often.

12.

*Babylon was a golden cup in the hand of the Lord, making the whole earth drunk; the nations drank of her wine, therefore the nations went **mad**.* Jeremiah 51:7

The Pursuit of Power (3)

Mad – The elixir of the gods is power. It is the aphrodisiac of self-sovereignty. And it is deadly. Jeremiah proclaimed that the world of the 6th Century BC was drunk on the power of Babylon. What do you think the world is drinking today? The same toxic brew has been spilling into the halls of government for as long as men have believed they are in charge of their destinies. *Today* is the 6th Century BC. We worship those who wield the sword, proclaim everlasting prosperity and devour the earth. We are the madmen, consuming ourselves in the rush to have more. We are a world of bigger barns, storing up our treasures here while God prepares an accounting for our souls. Oblivious of our impending doom, we reel from one barstool to another, leaving in our wake the vast sea of impoverished faces. Drinking to stay drunk in order not to face the guilt of our pointless excess, we transform the powerful into idols and role models while we vicariously live their unrighteous exploits.

Is the world mad? How else can it be described? In a headlong death spiral of disobedience, only insanity can account for the complete disregard of the awe of existence and the call of the Creator. Men are lauded for their rejection of the fundamental question, "What does God demand of me?" But this is not an inherited condition, although it is certainly passes from one generation to another. This is *voluntary* madness. It is not only completely unnecessary, it is also completely unexplainable. There is no *reason* for sin. Sin is insanity. It is the deliberate decision to destroy myself by ignoring the grace, peace and harmony that God offers. Why would anyone do that? The question presupposes there is a *valid* reason for such self-contradictory actions. There is no valid reason. There is only madness.

The choice of Hebrew word here is most instructive. It is *halal*, the same word that means "to praise" used in conjunction with ministry to God. *Halal* includes boasting, shouting, acting foolishly and raging insanity. Consider the spectrum here. On the same scale we find madness and godly praise. What is the difference? Only the object of our worship. To be in one's right mind is to be in praise of the one true God. To be insane is to be in praise of myself. Reasonable men, men of sound and righteous minds, are confronted with the inexplicable behavior and thought of madmen when they encounter those who are most surely running the path to self-destruction. There is no ground for argument or negotiation with such men. Until they come to their right minds, they are no different than the Gerasene demoniac, dangerous to themselves and to anyone in proximity. The Bible does not apply the terminology of the DSM IV to such men. It calls them demon-possessed for that is what they are. Insane. Self-destructive. Savage. Desperate.

Removing the spiritual component of such terminal behavior by dressing it in psychological garb is a mark of general cultural insanity. Redefining self-inflicted, eternal destruction as "normal" behavior does more to assist the enemy than any decline in morality. Men no longer fear the inevitable consequences of voluntary madness because today voluntary madness - the rejection of God's instructions - is *accepted and expected* even within the Church. The nations came to the table of the Eucharist and were offered intoxication. Now who's drunk?

13.

*Babylon was a golden cup **in the hand** of the Lord, making the whole earth drunk; the nations drank of her wine, therefore the nations went mad.* Jeremiah 51:7

The Pursuit of Power (4)

In The Hand – Babylon was an instrument in the hand of YHWH for His purposes. The text tells us quite clearly that the power of Babylon was no accident, no serendipitous political occurrence. It was *be-yad YHWH*, "in the hand of YHWH." He is the Master of history. Should we forget that, we will suffer the same stupor that accompanied the nations who drank Babylon's wine.

Did you notice that God Himself provided the golden cup that intoxicated the nations? His purposes were served in the dulled consciousness and drunken actions of the nations. Their alcoholic addiction to power provided the necessary environment for God's display of sovereignty. The nations did not fall simply because they were disobedient. They fell because God allowed them to pursue madness. He removed His protective shield. Without the Spirit's restraint, men became what they desired. *Yetzer ha'ra* directed their actions. But that does not mean the consequences did not serve God's purposes.

Jeremiah provides the proper response to this madness. "Wail for her; take balm for her pain; if perhaps she may be healed" (v. 8) for the Lord is about to bring vengeance (v. 6). "Do not be silenced by her iniquity" (v. 6). Suddenly, the distillery of the world's intoxication is broken. The barrels have split. The wine is spilled. Disaster peers from the horizon. What must the righteous do? Anything but remain silent!

Cry out to the Lord. Take pity on those who are about to expire. Offer healing wherever needed. Do something about this madness! Plead on behalf of the inmates that God might yet spare them. Perhaps God will turn away His wrath. Perhaps. Declare the righteousness of YHWH in Zion. Purify yourselves. Prepare for His victory.

We need Jeremiah today. Why? We need Jeremiah because we live in Babylon, that great empire that refused to acknowledge the sovereignty of the Lord. Because we live in such a place, we are removed from the blessings of His land – our land. We are strangers in a strange place, but we are not abandoned. Babylon is in our hand too. We are here to manifest His righteousness in a world gone mad. We are here to restrain drunken behavior, to resist addictions to power, to clean up the vomit of those whose indulgence exceeds their capacity. Silence is tantamount to sinful endorsement. Failure to act is the equivalent of faithlessness.

Today you will certainly encounter someone who is drunk on the wine of this godless culture. Your first reaction maybe one of revulsion and a desire to flee. But if you are to serve the purposes of the coming King, you must wail, plead, and heal. Today is the day. Tomorrow He comes.

14.

*The steps of a **man** are ordered from YHWH, and He will delight in his way. Though he falls, he will not be cast down, for YHWH upholds his hand.* Psalm 37:23-24

No One In Particular?

Man – It is certainly a shame that some English translations use the word "man" for the Hebrew *geber* in this verse. The KJV offers some help with its parenthetical expression "good" and the NLT provides "godly," but in general most English translations ignore the fact that this is not the Hebrew word *ish* or *adam*. We have seen these distinctions before (April 12 and May 16). In this verse, we really need to know the difference between these three Hebrew words. *Geber* is particularly important in David's use. These are the mighty men, the warriors, the ones of spiritual strength. Job uses the word fifteen times to distinguish the character of the *geber* from ordinary men. Most importantly, Zechariah 13:7 describes God as *geber* (a statement we will need to look at more carefully). The lesson is clear. Not every man has steps ordered by the Lord.

What kind of man is a *geber*? Let's see what Job suggests. A *geber* is:

A man-child, born perhaps for tests and trials (3:3)
A man whose way may be hidden from him by God (3:23)
A man who is just and pure (4:17)
A man who is aware of his mortality (10:5)
A man who knows he will certainly die (14:10)
A man who pleads with God (16:21)
A man who intercedes for a neighbor (16:21)
A man who is vigorous in usefulness to God (22:2)
A man who is wise and useful to himself (22:2)
A man who keeps from pride and turns aside from bad conduct (33:17)
A man who desires to be redeemed (33:39)
A man who may suffer in this life (34:7)
A man who understands there may be no profit when *he* is pleased with God (34:9)
A man of true understanding (34:34)
A man who is ready to take action (38:3)
A man who will answer to God (40:7)

Clearly not every man may have his steps ordered by YHWH.

Are these your characteristics? Do you see yourself in each of these descriptions from Job? Better yet, do *others* see you described by Job's words? If you find a few vacancies when you
apply Job's definition of *geber* to yourself, perhaps you need to reconsider what being a man really is. There are lots of men who are nothing more than male homo sapiens (*ish*). And all men (and women) are *adam*. But only a few are *geber*.

15.

*And Moses took the **blood** and sprinkled on the people and said, "Behold, the blood of the covenant which YHWH has cut with you concerning these things."* Exodus 24:8 (J. Green translation)

Blood Brothers

Blood – The New Testament authors lay emphasis on the blood of Yeshua. We now take it for granted that they are expressing the need for a blood sacrifice for the forgiveness of sin. We don't find their statements unusual or surprising. But maybe we should. A thorough examination of the relationship between blood and covenant in the Tanakh leads to this unexpected result. "The only verse which seems to hint at this directly is Exodus 24:8 with its reference to the application of blood to the participants, namely, the altar as the representative of God on the one side and the people on the other."[32] In spite of our common *assumption* that blood, sin, forgiveness and covenant are all tied together, there is only *one* verse in the entire Hebrew Scriptures that suggests this connection. Since blood sacrifice and covenant seem so important, we must ask why we only find this once.

To answer the question, we need to dig deeper into the background of Semitic tribal law. All of the cultures surrounding Israel practiced a form of covenant that was the basis of legal agreements between parties. Many of these practices involved rituals (like meals, oaths and physical symbols of the agreement – see Genesis 31:44 ff). Israel's covenants were not new. They were simply modified in some cases. These Semitic covenants seem to be

---

[32] Quell, *TDNT*, Vol. II, p. 115.

based first and foremost on *blood* relations. This helps us see why blood is part of the covenant between God and Israel. The blood of the covenant establishes a blood relation between God and His people. What this means in the Semitic world is that God and His people are now *one*! They are of the same family, tied together for eternity by blood. The symbolic use of blood sprinkled on the people and the altar establishes the unalterable, permanent, inviolable, legal connection. From this point forward, Israel is God's son and it is no more possible to break this relationship than it is to break the genealogical relationship between any father and son. Quell writes, "The most that we can say is that this material gives a certain plausibility to the view that even in the custom of Israel we are dealing with blood rites which have nothing to do with sacrifice but which are designed to establish a fellowship of substance between covenant partners."[33]

We will have to rethink the statements of the New Testament authors. If the covenant of blood is about establishing a familial relationship with YHWH, then the sacrifice of Yeshua must be about something else. God already established the blood relation at Sinai. No new relation was needed or necessary. God's family included *all* who participated in the covenant no matter how they happened to become part of it. So the sacrifice does not establish the covenant. The covenant is established by an oath of fidelity that God makes to Himself.

Two important conclusions can be drawn. First, God's covenant with Israel is as permanent as a father's genealogical connection to his son. There is *no possibility of a replacement*. Even if someone else is adopted as a son, the *blood relation* to the progeny of the father cannot be erased.

---

[33] Quell, TDNT, Vol. II, p. 115.

Second, the sacrifice isn't about this covenant. God does not establish our relationship to Him with sacrifice. The relationship is established with the oath of covenant. Sacrifice treats another matter. Understanding the Semitic background of covenant makes it even stronger for us. It also helps us look more closely at the purpose of sacrifice.

16.

Those who **trust** *in the LORD are as Mount Zion, which cannot be moved but abides forever.* Psalm 125:1

Eternal Security

Trust – Trusting YHWH doesn't matter until it matters. When life is consumed by the routine, we don't think much about trust. If we think of it at all, we think about the expectation of its consistency. I don't have to *trust* that the sun will come up tomorrow. I don't have to *trust* that tomorrow will be another day of writing or traveling or phone calls. Those things fall into the category of inevitability. They happen because the universe generally follows a cause and effect scenario. That's why I have an appointment calendar. Life is not normally chaotic.

Trust is important when life isn't so routine. That doesn't mean you have to have an externally observable crisis like a terrorist attack or the loss of your job or a devastating injury. Life can be chaotic on the inside too. It can be filled with doubts, fears, loneliness, heartache; things that are hidden from the observation of others but are quite apparent to the one feeling the chaos. While you might not need an example because you already know this experience, indulge me here. I am often afraid. Of course, I don't talk about my fears and I do my best not to show them publicly, but I know very well that they are there. I fear failure. I fear shame. I fear being left behind, being alone. Most of my fears are emotionally charged projections of self-induced despair. I simply don't think I'm good enough - for my wife, my family, my friends or for God. I have a long history of sins. I know guilt in the first degree. That's why *trust* is such a critically important *experience* for me.

I resisted writing that trust is a concept or an idea. Concepts and ideas will not remove the inner terror. I must *experience* trust to know it is real. Trust is found in behavior, not in dictionaries. If I hear my friend say, "Trust me," but I see him act in ways that appear to be irresponsible or personally damaging to me, his words become nothing but words. I might suggest that he become a politician but I probably won't give him my checkbook. This is even more critical when I have to deal with my most intimate inner fears. There has to be a *reason* to put confidence in someone and that reason cannot be a verbal assertion of fidelity.

But trust contains a paradox. In order to trust someone, I must take a risk. You see, no matter how much behavioral evidence I have that the other person is trustworthy, I know they might still fail me. I know this because I know myself and I have produced considerable evidence of trustworthiness and yet still failed to be 100% faithful. And if I can fail myself, others can also fail me. How can I really trust if trust requires me to *risk* what I don't trust?

The psalmist exhorts me to trust YHWH. But why should I? Have I seen His invisible hand moving in my life? Am I confident that He will shelter me from my personal terrors? Do I feel *safe* with Him? I certainly can't answer these questions with a resounding "Yes!" unless I have *experienced* His care and concern. But even if I have, there is this tendency to doubt His *continued* care, especially when I have no doubt at all about my sinfulness. This is when I need to know the difference between the Greek words for trust and the Hebrew word for trust.

Hebrew expresses trust with the word *batah* (*Bet-Tet-Chet*). The pictograph is "inside the surrounding fence." In other words, the principal idea behind trust is *protection*. Trust is expressed in *feeling* secure, in being able to rely on someone, in being unconcerned based on confidence in another. Hebraic trust is about feelings! It's not a lofty theological concept. It's real behaviorally-based emotional security. The most important words that I can say in any relationship are these: "I trust you." That means I place my well-being in your hands because I am confident that you are reliable, responsible and concerned about me. I believe that you will bring me *shalom*. If I don't believe these things, then no matter what I say, I don't trust you. When I say, "I trust you," I take the *risk* implied in the equation of trust. I hope that my risk is rewarded, but I don't know *for sure*. The Greeks noticed this inherent paradox, so their expressions of trust tend to be a little different than the Hebrew idea of security.

Greek doesn't have an exact equivalent for this feeling of inner safety. In the Greek New Testament, several different words are translated "trust," but none of them fits the Hebrew perfectly. Greek uses *elpizo* (to hope, to expect with desire), *peitho* (to convince, to persuade), *pepoithesis* (from *peitho* – trust or confidence), *pisteuo* (to believe, to have faith, to trust) and *proelpizo* (from *elpizo* – to see ahead, to know or foresee). You can see the *cognitive* orientation of the Greek terms in opposition to the *emotional* orientation of the Hebrew word. You can see that the basic idea of trust in Greek is tied to *hope*, not security. That doesn't mean the Greek expressions aren't correct. It just means that Hebrew is a "rubber meets the road" approach. In Hebrew, trust is about living, not just about thinking. In Hebrew, it's about what I am experiencing *now*, not what I wish to experience if everything works out the way I *hope* it will. Perhaps that's why we find this startling fact of the Hebrew Scripture: there are hardly any verses that actually describe people who trusted YHWH. There are plenty of verses that exhort us to trust Him but there are less than a dozen verses that tell us about people who *actually did* trust Him. Apparently the most important element of any relationship is not only difficult among human beings who can and do fail us, it is just as difficult with a God who never fails us. We might reflect on this fact when it comes to the lives of Yeshua's disciples. There is no doubt that Yeshua demonstrated His trustworthiness, but every disciple ran when put to the test.

Now we have discovered why trust requires such an effort. Others fail to uphold our trust. H̲avvah failed Adam. Adam failed H̲avvah. It's been the same ever since. Based on my experience with other people, I can never *completely* trust anyone. That is not a reflection of their deliberate malfeasance. It is simply a statement of the human condition. Everyone stumbles. I have failed to be trustworthy innumerable times. Just ask those who love me the most. I have failed to keep confidence *with myself.* Just ask God. So how can I trust someone else? They are just as human as I am. How can I put my well-being in the hands of someone else with *unconcern* for the consequences? In spite of the fact that the Bible exhorts me to place my well-being in the hands of my wife (Proverbs 31:11) in the same way that I would place my full confidence in YHWH, I struggle to do so because I have experienced pain and suffering at the hands of those I trusted. I am afraid because I know what it means to be double-crossed. To trust is to *risk* myself.

Paradox is at the heart of trust. Coming to grips with this paradox is the task of the human condition. I cannot become what God intends until I *risk* trusting Him and others. Other people may disappoint, but that cannot prevent me from risking myself with God. I must take myself by the neck and say, "What's the matter with you? God *doesn't fail.* Ever! It doesn't matter what the circumstances happen to be. He is completely trustworthy even if you can't figure out how He is engineering your life to bring about *shalom.* Stop peering in from outside the fence. Put your hand on the gate and step in. Of course it's scary.

But who are you to judge this situation? Is God like you? Not a chance! Put your fears away and take the risk to trust Him no matter where it goes. Put Him to the test. He's up to it."

17.

*The statutes of the Lord are **right**, rejoicing the heart; the commandment of the Lord is pure, enlightening the eyes.* Psalm 19:8 (Hebrew World translation)

Straight-Edge

Right – Take a piece of paper at least 10 inches wide. Now cut a perfectly straight line across that paper. I'll bet you can't do it without a straight-edge of some kind. Carpenters know all about this tool. So do seamstresses and engineers. Without a hard edge guide, our attempts to make straight cuts waver. The same principle applies to living. Without a hard edge alongside, the path wavers.

The Hebrew adjective *yashar* means straight, just or right. It can refer to both physical and ethical applications. Its root means "to go straight, to make right, to lead, to be made level, to be upright." Here we see the tangible grounding of Hebraic thought. What do the statutes of the Lord provide? A straight edge for life, a level that determines our alignment, a way of leadership, the standard of uprightness. What are these statutes? The word is *mitzvah*. It can mean human commands like those of a king, but in the Pentateuch (the first five books of the Bible) it is *always* applied to the commands of God.

Let's apply the psalmist's insight. In a world where men make their own standard, we find nothing but crooked paths. God's way is a hard, straight edge. If we want true leaders, we must look for those who adhere to His commands. Leadership is not about "vision casting." It is about strict obedience. Following a man who does not level his life according to God's commands is utter foolishness. When it comes to personal decisions, God's *mitzvah* set the standard. They provide us with the guide we need to stay on the path. They do not change. Whenever we find men and women who waver from His hard edge, we find ethical and moral chaos.

Notice that the result of a strict standard of straight action is *rejoicing*. Most people in the modern world would be surprised by the psalmist's choice here. They think of standards for moral actions as limitations or impediments. They don't rejoice over commands. They resist. They view God's straight edge as imposed obligation, not the way to freedom. Instead of rejoicing that God cares enough to offer a holy guide to living, they express bitterness or rebellion. They want the world to be shaped according to their idea of a straight line.

If you want to know who really loves the Lord, look for those who rejoice over His commands. Those who are gladdened by His instructions, those who love to follow His directions are the ones who truly love Him. They know that the straight edge keeps them on the right path. They look forward to correction. They want to cut the perfect line.

Examine yourself. Are you rejoicing over God's commands? Are you glad for His chastisement? Or is there a flaw in your ruler that you're not willing to smooth away?

18.

"Is it permissible to heal on the Sabbath?" Matthew 12:10

Don't Fence Me In

Permissible – The Sabbath is a day of rest, an honoring of God's creative effort and a fulfillment of His ordinance for our own good. But every Jew knew that the commandment concerning the Sabbath was part of a hierarchy of commandments, some of which were more important than others if the occasion ever arose where there was a conflict between commandments. Yeshua acknowledges this common understanding when He asserts that no man would leave his sheep in a pit on the Sabbath. Life matters more. Even today, hospitals are open in Jerusalem on Shabbat. Life is more important.

The question is not "Should I observe the Sabbath?" Yeshua *never* suggests we may ignore this commandment. The question is "How should I observe the Sabbath?" The debate with the Pharisees revolves around the extension of the biblical command found in the details of Pharisaic legal requirements. It's not that the Pharisees were simply being difficult. They were trying to cover all the possible conditions in order to give direction to the people so that there would be no mistakes in observance. This is called "building a fence around the Torah." The idea is to extend the commandment so that there is no possibility of even coming close to offending God. So, if there were a commandment not to walk more than two miles on Shabbat, the Pharisees might have a "fence" at one and one-half miles, just to make sure no one accidentally stepped over the two mile limit.

The need for fences is particularly important with the Sabbath. Why? Because the actual prohibitions found in Scripture for work on the Sabbath are sometimes pretty vague. Scripture prohibits the following:

1. gathering manna (Exodus 16:22-30)
2. gathering firewood (Numbers 15:32-36)
3. plowing and harvesting (Exodus 34:21)
4. kindling a fire (Exodus 35:3)
5. trading (Nehemiah 10:31, Amos 8:5)
6. carrying loads (Jeremiah 17:19-27)

The Mishnah Tractates *Shabbat* and *'Erubin* greatly expand these few guidelines under thirty-nine categories of what constitutes work. The Tractates are filled with lengthy discussions of the details. Living according to the Tractates involves a great deal more than simply following the biblical directives. Of course, the biblical directives are not specific, so questions will always arise about whether or not some specific action is really work. That's what this question (Is it permissible?) is all about. It's not a question about what is *obvious* from Scripture. It's a question about what the general categories given in Scripture mean when it comes to the details. For example, in Israel hotels have a "Shabbat" elevator because one school of interpretation considers pressing the button for a floor a version of kindling a fire (the button creates a spark in the electrical system). To avoid violating this commandment, the "Shabbat" elevator is programmed to stop on every floor without anyone touching a button.

Notice how Yeshua reacts to this question. He answers the Pharisees with another question. "Will a man rescue his only sheep from a pit if it falls in on the Sabbath?" The assumed answer is "Yes." If a human being is worth more than a sheep, then it is appropriate to heal on the Sabbath. Yeshua endorses a Torah hierarchy. He does not allow for flagrant violation, but He recognizes that there are circumstances where goodness and compassion set aside other considerations.

Most of us are not going to heal a man with a withered hand on Shabbat. If the occasion arises, we have a precedent to follow. Most of us are going to have to deal with apparently trivial matters, like sheep falling into pits. Our circumstances may be different, but the issue is still the same. What constitutes work? How would you answer that? Some actions are obvious. They are found in the Tanakh. Most are not obvious. For those we will have to do some serious reflection.

19.

*"He has **walled up** my way so that I cannot pass, and He has put darkness on my paths."* Job 19:8 NASB

Emotional Wreckage

Walled Up – The great difference between a believer and a non-believer is perspective. The non-believer's worldview is filled with help-myself actions. The prayers of non-believers are really attempts to get some divine entity to provide aid. These prayers may be quite a bit more sophisticated than the futile cries of the prophets of Ba'al, but they are no less motivated. Regardless of theological persuasion, people who try to bend God's ear to their desires would never appreciate Job.

185

Job has a believer's point of view. God is in charge, no matter what. We might not understand what He is doing, especially when it doesn't fit what we want Him to do, but that doesn't mean He has failed to meet our needs. God is good. That implies He determines what is good. Sometimes that makes it appear as if He stands in *opposition* to us. Steve Brown once told me that he doesn't doubt God's sovereignty at all, but he has a few issues with God's benevolence. I am pretty sure that unless you have struggled with this dilemma, you haven't yet embraced the full nature of faith. Ultimately faith is not about what I think God is doing or even what He reveals to me about what He is doing. Ultimately faith is about trusting who He is – and being content with the outcome.

Of course, contentment doesn't come easily. Contentment is the result of *struggle*, not passive acceptance. This means faith is exhibited by **interaction with God**, even if that interaction is argument, frustration, complaint or demands. The perspective of the believer is that God is in the mix – entirely. The non-believer simply acts as if God is in the mix occasionally, whenever He is needed. In other words, the believer's world is filled with God issues. The non-believer's world is filled with personal issues. The believer struggles with the world because he knows God is active in everything. The non-believer struggles with the world because he thinks God *isn't* active in everything.

Job knows God has walled him up. Not circumstances. Not fate. Not sin. Not mistakes. All those are simply rationalizations or diversions. The issue is God. That is always the issue. God *interferes* in the life of a believer. His interference isn't always pleasant or benevolent, but it is always purposeful.

If God is interfering with you, you are in good company. If you think you need to ask for God's interference, you probably haven't engaged Him as you should. Take a lesson from Job. <u>Emotional wreckage is a sign of divine involvement.</u> *Gadar* (to close up, to wall off) is God therapy in action. Lie back on the couch and let Him go to work.

20.

*My people are destroyed from lack of knowledge. Because you have rejected knowledge I will **reject you** from priestly service for me. You have forgotten the instruction of your God; so I too will forget your children.* Hosea 4:6 (translation J. A. Dearman)

For Whom the Bell Tolls (1)

Reject you – We feel good about the love story of Hosea. In spite of Gomer's unfaithfulness, Hosea redeems her and restores her. As a metaphor for Israel, we rejoice that God's faithfulness wins in the end. But maybe we are too quick to rush to the conclusion. Maybe the process of redemption is so painful, so full of risk and warning that we gloss over the terror in the text. That would be a mistake. All the words are God's words. So, sit down. Take a deep breath and listen to the alarm. The bell tolls for you and me.

Whom does God reject? We could opt for the easy answer. God rejects the false priests. God rejects those who teach heresy or lead His people astray. God rejects those who fail to act upon His instructions. Of course, that's not us. We are the good people of God. We can dismiss this verse. It doesn't apply.

But what if there is more in mind here? What if God is

rejecting the leaders of His people who reject His instruction and, as a result, God is also rejecting those who follow them? Take one step back and ask yourself why God established Israel in the first place. Didn't God constitute Israel to be a royal priesthood to the nations? Doesn't that mean that everyone who claims to be called by His name but rejects His instruction is rejected as a priest to the nations? It's not just the leaders who are in the crosshairs. We who claim to follow are also targets of God's rejection. We cannot be priests if our leaders do not remember (bring to mind for action) *and* we do not fulfill His instructions.

"I will reject you" (*em-aska*) encompasses both the leadership and the followers. The root (*ma'an*) describes the refusal of an offer. In pictograph, chaos confronts life – and wins. God's order is withdrawn. Life devolves. The people of God *collectively* stumble and fall. No one escapes the consequences of a failure of leadership. If you thought that your obedience would keep you safe in a community that fails to bring God's instructions into action, be warned. The bell tolls for you.

Why does God reject? Hosea is a story of recovery. Why would God pronounce rejection? The answer is obvious: measure for measure. The leaders reject God's wisdom. They refuse God's offer of order. The rejection might come as a result of forgetting or ignoring or rebellion. It doesn't matter. Measure for measure. The leaders bring the consequences upon themselves. God refuses them. The real tragedy is that the leaders carry the people. They literally hold the welfare of the people in their hands. Rejection of God's ways has direct consequences on *all* the followers. The people are rejected by God, not because they are immediately responsible, but because their leadership has failed. No man can survive the judgment of God once he enlists in the service of leaders who reject the wisdom of the

King. I guess the important question is this: Who am I following?

21.

*My people are destroyed from lack of knowledge. Because you have rejected knowledge I will reject you from priestly service for me. You have **forgotten** the instruction of your God; so I too will **forget** your children.* Hosea 4:6 (translation J. A. Dearman)

For Whom the Bell Tolls (2)

Forget – When you think of the Hebrew verb forget, think of Robert Frost, the American poet. "Fences make good neighbors," wrote Frost. In Hebrew, *shakah* does much more than make good neighbors. To forget is to tear down the fence that provides life. The pictograph of *Shin-Kaf-Chet* is "what destroys the fence around the open palm." God fences us in on purpose. The broken world is a dangerous and unhealthy place. God protects with His instructions, often in ways that we cannot comprehend. When we *forget*, we tear down the fence that keeps life and chaos apart. When we forget, we let sin in. When we forget, we open the door (as Paul says) and life tumbles.

You'll say, "I haven't forgotten the Lord. I pray. I read my Bible. I am involved in a believing community. God is real to me." Wait a minute. Let's step back and take a deeper look at this verse. Of course, these are words of the prophet Hosea to Israel, so in the historical sense it isn't written to us. But the principle applies. We can experience the destitution of silence if we reject the Way. There is something here for us in spite of the fact that the words are thousands of years old. Here is the principle: "measure for measure." Forgetting works both ways. If we forget, God forgets. Now look closely at what we are likely to forget (and what Israel is accused of forgetting). Hosea doesn't say, "You have forgotten *Me!*" That would be a non sequitur. If the people actually forgot *God*, then His words to them would be like hearing thunder in the distance. Who knows what that means? No, YHWH says, "You have forgotten *My instructions!*" Now we have specificity. Now we know exactly what has happened. These people claim to follow YHWH but they do not do what YHWH tells them to do. The bell tolls for them, not because they don't have a "relationship" but because they don't act according to the obligations of the relationship. They have a "saving knowledge" but their lives are examples of sinful acts. Consequently, they are forgotten.

We learn a very important linguistic (and spiritual) lesson here. The opposite of forgetting is not remembering. The opposite of forgetting is obeying. In the cognitive world of Greek epistemology, forgetting is a *mental* state. Therefore, its antonym is also a mental state. In the Greek world, forget is the opposite of remember. But in Hebraic metaphysics, forgetting is not about a mental condition. It is about a moral failure. To forget is to tear down the fence between chaos and life. Forgetting is failing to bring something into action. Forgetting is the failure to *respond* to the demands of the Lord. It's not mental. It's moral.

Now we can ask ourselves if we have forgotten God. How? By comparing our lives with the standard of His instructions. Where we find a mismatch, forgetting should come to mind. ☺ Check out the 613 for starters. If you want to see the rest of the obligations, take a look here. You might be surprised to find that there are *more* commands in the New Testament than there are in the Torah. Then ask yourself if you are remembering or forgetting.

22.

*In a place where there are **no people**, strive to be a man.*
Rabbi Hillel *Pirke Avot* 2:6B

Being Human

No People – Hillel's saying is not an endorsement of the monastic life. He is not suggesting that we strive to become truly human in the wilderness. What Hillel means is this: there are plenty of communities where human beings exist but are not really persons. They live according to the impetus of their desires. They are subject to the winds of circumstance. They survive – but they do not thrive as partners in God's restoration of the world. They are not truly human beings as God intended. They are missing the joy of being. In those places (and they are all around us), strive to be what God intended persons to be – fully human, the bridge between heaven and earth.

Does this mean your focus is concentrated on the spiritual appetites? Are you to be in constant meditation, memorizing your Bible, saying your prayers, walking with your hands lifted up to heaven? No. The rabbis realized that *involvement* in community, *compassion* for others and a deep sense of *awe* are the supreme characteristics of truly human existence. As followers of Yeshua HaMashiach, we don't have to look any further than His story to see just how much these three elements impact the lives of those in His presence. We are called to be the same kind of *engaged person*, wherever we happen to be. Hillel exhorted his *talmidim* to strive to become men of God. Yeshua invites us to *come after Him*. The result is nearly the same.

Berkson notes, "When you maintain concern for the people you work with and for the community, and try to serve their needs, you build the kind of relationships that benefit you in the long run."[34] Being truly human not only blessed others; it benefits you as well. Wasn't God clever to design it that way?

There is a significant leadership principle implied in this rabbinic statement – and in the parallel statements of Yeshua. Leaders who strive to be truly human will achieve that goal *only insofar as they serve those around them.* A leader is not the head of the pack because he is out front. He is only out front because others are willing to follow. One must be *invited* to be a leader. That occurs when the *talmidim* recognize the benefits of being followers. A leader who is not serving his followers is soon standing alone.

Yeshua never compels anyone to follow. His approach is always an invitation, an appeal to the *benefits* derived by the relationship with Him. Yeshua does not shy away from the *self-interest* of those who would come after Him. He knows that there are no followers unless there is perceived benefit. And He is more than willing to give benefits. Perhaps we would make a much greater impact on the community if we simply realized that being God's man or woman means *benefitting* those nearby. If we are going to strive to make a difference, it will begin by asking, "How can I serve you today?"

23.

*I have trodden the winepress **alone**.* Isaiah 63:3 (A. Heschel translation)

Alone – "It is not good for man to be alone," but on some occasions it is essential. "Proximity to the crowd, to the

---

34 William Berkson, *Pirke Avot*, p. 70.

majority view, spells the death of creativity. For a soul can create only when alone, and some are chosen for the flowering that takes place in the dark avenues of the night. They may live on the edge of despair, alternating between longing for fellowship and privacy."[35]

As a general rule, God calls us to community. But some He calls to a much more difficult existence. Some He calls to experience His abandonment. Some He calls to enter into the life of the divine divorce that He knows. Some He calls to empathize with Him. The edge of true creativity is the blade that cuts and spills our blood in the process of separation. It is safe in the crowd. It is comforting to walk in lock-step with the masses. But conformity does not produce depth or spiritual keenness or compassion. For that, we must suffer rejection, misunderstanding and fight the darkness within. No man or woman chooses this blithely. The cost is much too high. No prophet longed for the job. To push the envelope of the creative image of God in us is to risk being sacrificed "for the greater good." God Himself trod the wine press alone.

The Hebrew text expresses this form of existential abandonment with the combination of the preposition le and the adjective bad. This combination means "by itself" or "apart from." You will find an expression of the burden of this condition in Genesis 2:18. Here God Himself declares that He alone will bring the judgment upon Israel. He alone will be polluted by their blood. He alone accepts responsibility. In fact, the Hebrew emphasizes this solitary culpability by adding the suffix letter yod. "I, I alone have trodden the winepress."

The agony of being alone, in spite or because of the creative

---

[35] Abraham Heschel, A Passion for Truth, p. 215.

energy that brings about our destiny, is often too much to bear. We capitulate to the need for comfort and companionship and in the process we abdicate. Perhaps that is why there are so infinitely few who truly create while there are so many whose production is at best xerography. To come under the scalpel of creativity always leaves visible scars. There is no plastic surgery for genius.

God knows what it means to be alone. Since God is the most creative being, His depth of understanding exceeds any agony we might encounter in our expression of inspiration. While the consolation of His empathy does not replace the communal bliss of humanity, it at least can sustain us when we tread the winepress of imagination. He has been there before us. Rejection is His middle name.

To be alone might not be good, but there is good company when we are there.

Excursus
The Reluctant Leader

None of the above – voting for the one who doesn't want the job.

In the clamor of the call for leadership we often overlook one dramatic fact about biblical leaders. None of them wanted the job! Prophets, evangelists, priests, even the anointed ones often express great dismay over God's assignment. Moses tries several excuses in order to avoid the calling. Jeremiah wishes he has never been born. Even Yeshua has a time of great agony over the road that lies ahead of Him. The message seems abundantly clear: men and women who battle for the position of leader are probably the least likely of God's choosing.

God chooses those who are keenly aware of their inadequacies. God does so because these biblical leaders are less likely to lift themselves up with accumulated credit. In other words, pride is so dangerous to true leadership that God seeks the *humble* and the *humiliated* in order to accomplish His purposes. These characteristics are almost exactly the opposite of the factors human beings desire in leaders. If we understand the biblical point of view, we should see nothing but red flags surrounding those who want to be king, even if only king for a day!

Great men of God have recognized this paradox. It is worth listening to their voices on the matter. Here's what Abraham Heschel penned concerning warnings to leaders:

"Never show partiality either to yourself or to others. He who seeks the path of Truth will not make a good mixer or fellow traveler."[36]

"If you want to engage yourself to God, then you must sever yourself from the world as personified by society. Make no deals with it. You cannot be in love with both God and the world, dance at two weddings at once. What the world may endorse, conscience must often condemn."[37]

"Indebtedness expresses the pathos of being human, an awareness of the self as committed. Man cannot think of himself as human without being conscious of his indebtedness. Thus it is not a mere feeling but a constitutive feature of being human. To eradicate it would be to destroy man's humanity."[38]

"This sense of indebtedness is translated by people in a variety of ways: duty, obligation, allegiance, conscience, sacrifice. And the content and direction of each of these terms are subject to interpretation.

There is no authenticity in human existence without a sense of indebtedness, with an awareness that man must transcend himself, his interests, and his needs, without the realization that existence involves both utilization and celebration, satisfaction and exaltation.

All searching for rational meaning must yield to the reality upon which Judaism is built: to live is to obey. So many of us are haunted by the ugly futility of human effort, the triumph of brute force, of evil, and man's helpless misery. Is not any form of hopefulness false, unreal, self-deceiving?

---

[36] Abraham Heschel, *A Passion for Truth*, p. 227

[37] Abraham Heschel, *A Passion for Truth*, p. 228

[38] *Ibid.*, pp. 259-260.

What is Truth as available to us? Is it a curse, a path toward defeat laden with torment? Are we doomed to live with delusion while searching for Truth in vain? We spend a lifetime looking for the key, and when we find it, we discover that we do not know where the lock is." [39]

"One thing we can be sure of: the king has hired us, and the original responsibility is his. What we must do is to remember Him Who has engaged us."

"No Job arose in Hellas. Indeed, his outcry is part of the drama in which God and man are involved with one another." [40]

"Religious truth must be lived. A law unrelated to life is both futile and fatal to faith. Rigidity and love of life cannot always be reconciled.

Gone for our time is the sweetness of faith. It has ceased to come to us as a gift. It requires 'blood, sweat, and tears.' We are frightened by a world that God may have already abandoned. What a nightmare ot live in a cosmic lie, in an absurdity that makes pretensions to beauty."[41]

" . . . in a world of lies the demonic has free reign."[42]

The greatest danger for leaders is the fact that there are followers. Pushed by followers who idolize but do not comprehend the agony, the sacrifice and the constant

---

[39] *Ibid.*, pp. 287-288.

[40] Abraham Heschel, *A Passion for Truth*, p. 290.

[41] *Ibid.*, p. 320.

[42] *Ibid.*, p. 321

requirement for war against the power of self-deception, many leaders succumb to the accolades of the crowd, and in so doing remove God's hand from their destinies.

I have recommended several books to those who ask, "What should I do to become a leader?" None are found on the shelves of bookstores under the heading "Leadership," but unless the man or woman of God embraces the wisdom in these words, he or she is likely to look in the mirror one day and realize that all the has been accomplished is *hevel hevalim*, vanity, chasing after wind.

Books for Reluctant Leaders

1. *Love Not the World* – Watchman Nee
2. *Authority and Submission* – Watchman Nee
3. *The Way of the Heart* – Henri Nouwen
4. *In the Name of Jesus* – Henri Nouwen
5. *God of Weakness* – John Timmer
6. *The Making of a Man of God* – Alan Redpath
7. *The Practice of the Presence of God* – Brother Lawrence
8. *Money and Power* – Jacques Ellul
9. *Ruthless Trust* – Brennan Manning
10. *Your Money or Your Life* – John Alexander

Work and Worship
When Delight and Blessing Marry

What happens to being human when we separate work and worship? You may never have asked that question. You may have simply assumed that work and worship are completely separate functions, just like the popular myth that the functions of the state must be separated from religion. But now that we have raised the question, perhaps some reflection will give us insights into the biblical view of the integration of work and worship (and subsequently, the unification of the state and religion). The common proclamation concerning marriage ("what God had joined let no man separate") needs to be applied to our understanding of what we do and whom we worship. God joined these two together before He joined husband and wife. The fusion of our tasks in the world with our awe and reverence for the one who created the world is a fundamental principle of the Hebraic worldview. In fact, the same Hebrew word, *avad*, is used to describe what we do, whom we serve and whom we worship. Just as *shema* is both hearing and obeying, *avad* is both doing and worshipping.

This shift in perspective highlights the enormous conflict that we create for ourselves when we employ two distinct paradigms for work and worship. In the biblical world, there is no difference between Sunday and Monday (to put it in Christian terms), between the Sabbath and the rest of the week. Certainly, Shabbat is a day of rest. Tasks that I normally do on the other days are not to be done on Shabbat. But that rest is part of the pattern *avad*. What I do on the other six days is just as much honoring and glorifying YHWH as Shabbat. The idea that my religious life is confined to a specific day, or even to a few hours of that day, is an invention of the Western isolation of sacred and profane. God intended us to be fully functioning worshipping doers in every part of life. The only difference is that one day of week (on the Sabbath) we set aside those other worshipping tasks in order to honor the one who put the pattern in place in the beginning.

Now you can ask yourself, "Do I truly worship in my work?" It doesn't matter if you are a store clerk, an IT manager, a schoolteacher or the CEO of a multi-national corporation. Work must be a form of worship. What you do must, at the same time, honor the God who made you. Work isn't something you do in order to earn money so that you can go on vacation and do what you really wish you could do all the rest of the time that you are at work. *avad* is an expression of the way God made you to function in the world. That means what you do gives hands and feet to who He is. As soon as work is disassociated from the purpose God make for you, it becomes *toil*. It is no longer the integration of my true purpose and design under the umbrella of God's intention for me in the world. Since men have separated work and worship for centuries, it should be no surprise that most people *hate what they do*. Given the choice, they would abandon the toil they experience and become the person of their dreams. But reality stands in the way. The world embraces a paradigm that opposes the integration of work and worship. Understanding *why* this is true and what can be done about it is the first step in releasing us from a self-made prison.

The biblical world is a world that rests. It rests because it believes that God is sovereign, that God's purposes prevail, that self-determination is a failure to worship the Creator and a form of idolatry. The biblical world rests because it is not all up to me. Work and worship lead to humility, comfort and hope. There is a reason why we cannot serve two masters. One is a tyrant of our own making, determined to destroy us from the inside out.

1.

*"No man can **serve** two masters; for either he will hate the one and love the other, or he will hold to one and despise the other."* Matthew 6:24

Gender Idolatry

Serve – Yeshua is pretty clear about divided loyalty. No one, man or woman, can serve two masters. The Greek word used here is *douleuo*, a verb that literally means to take the position of a servant, a *doulos*, a slave. No one is able to accept slavery to two different authority figures.

Most of the time, we apply this famous verse to the issue of materialism. We act as though the subsequent remark, "You cannot serve God and mammon," is the only application of this verse. But that is foolish. Yeshua doesn't restrict the principle to finances. He merely makes one application of the general principle. Divided loyalty doesn't work.

Katherine Bushnell provides what I consider the final closing argument about the position of husbands and wives by applying this general principle to the case of marriage. If no one can serve two masters, then it follows that no woman can serve two authority figures as the same time. A woman *cannot* be in subjection to her husband *and* be in subjection to God. The same general principle applies. She will love one and despise the other; hold on to one and hate the other. Clearly, Yeshua expected every follower to recognize the foolishness of this division and put loyalty to Him ahead of everything else. This is no less the case in marriage. A woman who *serves* her husband as a slave (*douleuo*) *cannot* be God's slave, and a man who insists on a wife's obeisance stands in opposition to the command of the

Lord. When Paul and Peter exhort wives to submit to their husbands, they simply cannot mean wives should act as their husbands' slaves. That would violate everything Scripture teaches about the proper relationships with the Lord. If the principle is true about money, it is all the more true about relationships.

This tells us that submission is not servility. It is not about "who's in charge here," or "who's the *head* (authority) of the house." Submission must be something other than a hierarchy of slave service. We are all enjoined to submit to one another as unto the Lord, so whatever submission means, it must apply equally to both husbands and wives. It cannot be about an authority hierarchy or it would fall under the two-masters indictment.

What does it mean to *serve* from an Old Testament perspective? The Hebrew word is *avad*, the word for work, serve and worship. God Himself uses this verb when He instructs Pharaoh to let the people go so that they might *serve* Him. Now we see the bigger picture. My service to God is my work and my worship. With this in mind, no husband can possibly insist that his wife *serve* him. That would require the wife to *worship* her husband. It's time to stop this gender idolatry. The partners in a new covenant redeemed marriage do not endorse or demand an idolatrous hierarchy. They act as one on their way back to the Garden.

2.

And YHWH Elohim took the man and put him into the garden of Eden to **work** *it and to keep it.* Genesis 2:15

Passionate Productivity

Work – What kind of work do you do? I'm not asking about your occupation. I mean what is the relationship between what you do and who you are. What category of work do you fall into? Let me explain.

There are three categories of work. The first is work driven by compulsion. This is work that you are forced to do. Israel in Egypt worked under the compulsion of the Egyptian slave masters. Forced labor divides us from our tasks. We become human machines – replaceable, expendable, useful only for economic value. Not many of us work under compulsion, but we certainly know what it means.

The second category of work is driven by obligation. This is work that we voluntarily do in order to meet other needs. It is work we would rather not do, but which has to be done. If we didn't need the reward of our effort, we would forego the labor. This category encompasses *most* occupational engagements today. If we won the lottery, we would walk away from the job. Surveys report that nearly 70 % of Americans "hate" their work. They are laboring in obligation. They need the money. It's what they do to survive, but it isn't who they are. Oh yes, and if you spend your days in the work of obligation, you are on the path to burnout. Even your body was not designed to work this way.

The last category of work is passion. This is work that springs from the center of who we really are. This is work we were "born" to do. Amazingly, passion seems to be at the center of work that really drives change and really makes a difference in civilization. Without passion, work is merely a means to an end. But with passion, work is the end in itself. When we work passionately, we express something deep within us. We are energized by working rather than being exhausted by laboring. The effort is its own reward.

What category describes the work God gave Adam? Well, if God put Adam in the garden of God's delight, we can be pretty sure that the work Adam was supposed to do was not done out of compulsion or obligation. God gave Adam *passionate* employment. What Adam did to work and care for God's garden actually energized, fulfilled and satisfied Adam. He was "born" to the task. We can think of this as a slight variation on John Piper's famous quotation, "God is most glorified in us when we are most satisfied in Him." When it comes to passionate employment in the garden of God's delight, we are most satisfied when God is most glorified in the exercise of what we were made to do.

The Hebrew word here is *avad*. It is a familiar term, meaning work and serve, connected directly to the idea of worship. When we do what God has designed us uniquely to do - what is at the heart of our passion - our work becomes His service and an act of worship. The pictograph reveals "the path to the tent of the father." Passionate work brings me closer to God, back to the garden, to His tent of delight.

How tragic (and how subtle) for the enemy to convert what God intended as an expression of delightful energy into labor or compulsion. Do you remember what God told Adam after the Fall? "From this point on, your work will become labor. Your passion, what I made you for, will be laced with obligation." And so it is today.

Think about your work life. Are you laboring under obligation, caught in the rat-race of return? Are you moving toward passion-driven delight? Are you honoring God in *all* you do?

3.

*"And when you **pray**, you are not to be as the hypocrites . ."*
Matthew 6:5

Out Of The Box

Pray – We all agree that prayer is essential for a deep relationship with the Father. Almost all of us would say that we need to pray more. But far too often we stumble around in prayer. We don't have the clear, crisp, preacher voice, extolling God's virtues in a magnificent display of rhetoric. Our prayers seem insipid and weak. We're distracted. Our thoughts wander. We turn to the common categories of prayer in order to find direction. I am quite sure you are familiar with the acronym ACTS – Adoration, Confession, Thanksgiving and Supplication. If that doesn't seem to be enough, there are other classifications available: petition, prayers of intercession, prayers of penitence, prayers of thanksgiving, and prayers of adoration.

All of these are helpful, but I think they miss the point. Greek has basically one or two words for prayer (and a few extra tangents). English has one word. But Hebrew has more than two dozen. Furthermore, the idea of *classifying prayer* is quite Greek. Classification is about getting the right prayers in the right boxes so everything will be neat and tidy. Then we have a formula to follow, a pattern to practice. A few words of adoration, followed by a quick confession, some thanksgiving and then on to supplication. We know we have prayed *correctly* when we have included *all* the categories.

Can I be rather bold here? What was Yeshua's complaint about the hypocrites? They followed ritualized prayer. They had their formulae and patterns. They thought prayer was about covering all the bases. Are we any different? We say the ritual blessings. We repeat the "Lord's Prayer." We make sure we have the right pattern. In fact, when we don't pray like this, we are apt to think we aren't praying effectively. Book after book, lesson after lesson tries to get us into categorized praying. But when we look at the Hebrew Scriptures, we see something very different. We see prayer as *flow*.

In Hebrew, prayer includes weeping, shouting, dancing, clapping, growling, pleading, rejoicing, praising, asking, arguing, questioning, meditating, repeating, reveling, working, walking, complaining, confessing, worshipping, thanking, acknowledging, delighting, exalting, forgiving, boasting and more. What ties all these participles together? Living! Prayer is God's breath of life exhaled back to Him. It is the *flow* of living as He intended. It is the moment-by-moment consciousness of His presence in *everything* that affects me.

"When you pray," says Yeshua, "don't pray like those who use ritual, category, outward exhibition, proper eloquence or any other substitute for just being alive. Come to your Father as you are and enjoy being with Him."

4.

*"For this commandment which I command you today is **not too difficult** for you, nor is it out of reach."* Deuteronomy 30:11

Wonderful Obligations

Not Too Difficult – Moses instructed the people. His instructions are only part of the Torah. The stories of Adam, Noah, Abraham and Joseph are also Torah. They are narrative instructions. They provide us with living examples of how to live and how not to live. They are case studies in grace, mercy, sin and punishment. But one thing Moses makes crystal clear (in Hebrew) is this: it's a wonderful obligation!

Did you think Torah was rules and regulations? Is it just a long list of things you have to do once you are grafted into the commonwealth of Israel? If that's your frame of mind, then you haven't understood Torah at all. You need a lesson in Hebrew vocabulary. It can start right here with the phrase *lo niphlet* (not too wonderful-difficult). Yes, that's right. The root word *pala* (the "p" becomes "ph" in this derivation) means both "wonderful" and "difficult." Well, almost. You see, the root is a verb, not a noun. So it really means "to do something wonderful or difficult." Keeping Torah is doing something wonderful. But it is not difficult. That's where *lo* comes in. There are two negatives in Hebrew – *lo* and *al*. *Lo* is usually associated with absolutes like the absolute prohibitions of the Ten Commandments. On the other hand, *al* is often conditional, like the conditional prohibitions found in Proverbs. Which negative is used here? *Lo* – the one that says keeping His commandments is *absolutely* not too difficult.

OK, so God doesn't give us instructions for living that we cannot possible fulfill. What makes these same instructions wonderful? For that answer we need a bit of meditation on the nature of the Torah.

First, Torah is God's way of life. You don't have to follow a process of trial and error in order to know how to live. God spells it out for you. How simply *wonderful* is that? God takes all the guesswork out of living and makes it about as simple as it can be. Just do what He says.

Second, God *chooses* to give us His instructions. He didn't have to do that. He could have said, "Well, you made your choice. Now go figure it out yourself." But He didn't. He was merciful. He knew we were incapable of seeing the bigger reality of what it true and good and beautiful. So, He told us. Wonderful!

Third, living according to Torah is a blessing. It's not rule behavior. It's the privilege of honoring God by fulfilling His instructions. It's a form of worship. Wonderful! Now you know why a Jewish man can pray, "Lord, I thank you for not making me a woman." It's not misogyny. He thanks God because there are *more* commandments for men than there are for women and this means, as a man, he is able to honor and bless God more.

Finally, Torah is wonderful because applying it to my life makes me a light to the nations. I am different. I live differently. I think differently. I react differently. I am the salt that preserves God's way in the world. I am the light that attracts the world to Him. I am His representative on earth. Absolutely wonderful!

5.

but rather let him labor, working the good with the hands, that he may **have to give** *to the one having need.* Ephesians 4:28

Capitalism On Purpose

Have To Give – Why do you work? Try making the list of your work objectives. Let's see – pay the bills, keep a roof over your head, provide for your family, gain recognition for your efforts, do what you love to do (and get paid for it). You might add one more. Paul implies that one of the reasons for working is *to have in order to give.* The Greek phrase is *eche metadidomai.* This is capitalism on purpose. Why? Because the biblical view is giving from excess, that is, giving from the profit made above what is necessary to live. You have to *have* something before you are able to *give* it away.

210

There are a few implications here that require articulation. First, work is good. God established the goodness of work in the Genesis account. Work is part of what it means to become human. Of course, in God's design, work is supposed to be an expression of my true essence. I am designed by God to do exactly what fits His plan. When I work in that way, my work is a form of worship. It is fulfilling for me, delightful to Him and a blessing to others, all at once. If that's not what you're doing, it's time to reevaluate.

Secondly, work is not about accumulating. I do not have in order to have. It's not about collecting assets or toys. Work is designed to be the super-fruit of my life. I produce what God has designed me to produce for the benefit of others. My work becomes the vehicle for others' consumption. In the past, we looked at the idea that what I bear in my life becomes food for other lives. In this way, we are all interdependent on each other and dependent on the Lord.

Finally, we should notice that this verb, *metadidomi*, is used to describe the action of giving alms. It is about sharing what I have with someone in need. In other words, Paul suggests that work is intended to produce charity. This was enormously important in the Jewish community. From a biblical point of view, people do not work to enhance their lives. They work in order to live *so that* they may study Torah, pray and give to others. In this way, work becomes an act of righteousness. Maybe we need to do a quick evaluation of our attitudes and objectives when it comes to work. Outside the biblical culture, the objective of work is too often all about getting ahead, maintaining a lifestyle and collecting security for the future. All of those objectives rest on the basis of a world that needs to be controlled. Maybe you and I have unconsciously absorbed some of these misdirected goals. Maybe we need to take a long look at why we work and ask ourselves if *eche metadidomai* is at the top of our list.

6.

*O LORD, why do You **cause** us to stray from Your ways and harden our heart from fearing You?* Isaiah 63:17

The God of Good and Evil

Cause – How difficult it is to think that God causes us to stray! How can it be possible? How can Isaiah, the inspired prophet, tell us that God stands behind our disobedient wanderings? We want to throw up our hands and shout, "NO!" God can't be like this. He is good. He cannot be tempted. He rejects evil. So, why does Isaiah say something so terrible?

When we look carefully at this verse, we find that the verb *ta'ah* (to wander, to err, to go astray) is in a verb form that implies causation. In other words, there really isn't any word like "cause" in this text. The verb itself implies that God causes this action. Isaiah uses the same verb in 53:6, "All we like sheep have gone astray. . ." Of course, in this passage in Isaiah, we are the ones who are responsible for this situation. But here Isaiah seems to suggest that God is responsible. It's a problem.

It's a problem until we realize how Hebrew works. Hebrew is a phenomenological language. It describes how things appear. It is the language of observation, not analysis. Now consider Isaiah's statement. Aren't there times when it certainly *appears* as if God is making life a twisted mess? Don't we sometimes feel *as* *if* God is behind our disobedience? We certainly blame Him for things, don't we? Aren't there days when we want to shout, "God, why did you make me do this? You're sovereign over all things. Your plans never fail. But look at me. I have wandered away from You. Didn't You *know* that this would happen? Of course You did! So, why did You let it happen? Why didn't You stop me?" At those moments we might use the same words Isaiah uses. "You, O YHWH, cause us to stray and You have hardened our hearts."

If we read this with Greek eyes, we think of the statement as incompatible with the goodness of God. We see theological conflict. We see contradiction. We don't see how it is logically possible to say that God is good and, in the same breath, say that He causes evil. But Isaiah does say this. He says it because he is recounting what appears to be the case, especially for men who would love to shift the blame to the Creator. Oh, does that remind you of a certain situation in Genesis? "Look, Lord, I'm not to blame here. You made this woman. You gave her to me. I followed her lead. I just did what I was supposed to do. It's not my fault." Maybe we haven't really come very far from the gates of Eden after all.

Biblical Hebrew portrays a story written from the eyes of the beholder. Sometimes we need to be reminded about that particular perspective. The Bible doesn't come to us as a neutral dissertation on theological doctrines. It comes to us clothed in human observation, filled with specifically human proclivities. When we read it, we need to account for the "human factor," just as God does when He speaks to us through it. It's not such a strange book after all. It's just God telling us in our language. If God can do that, then I suppose we can speak to Him in the same language, can't we? Just tell Him the way it is, the WYSIWYG (What You See Is What You Get) way, and see what happens.

7.

For not the hearers of the law are justified with God but the **doers** *of the law shall be justified.* Romans 2:13

Order-Takers

Doers – This is a nearly impossible verse for Augustine and Luther (and those who follow their lead). It's impossible because Paul unequivocally says that those who *do* the commandments of God are justified. Actually, it's even worse than that. Paul says that those who merely *hear* God's commandments but do no do them are not justified. This is about as strong a statement about the necessity of following God's instructions in Torah as you will find in the New Testament. And it comes from the apostle of "grace." What can we say?

A quick look at the Greek confirms the dilemma. The word is *poietes*, from the verb "to make" (*poieo*). It clearly means someone who performs the required commandments. There's not much wiggle room here. Paul says it plainly: justification comes from keeping the commandments.

This conclusion is so antithetical to the long-standing Christian doctrine of *sole fide, sole gratia* that we are apt to do whatever we can to reinterpret Paul's statement. Unfortunately, we don't take Paul seriously. We retain the paradigm rather than recognizing that something doesn't make sense. It isn't Paul who is confused. It's our interpretive scheme. Thanks to Augustine, the early church fathers, the Reformers and the evangelicals, we would rather believe what we want to believe than listen to the apostle. Paul doesn't see conflict. Grace and works form a covenant *together*. We are the ones who split them apart – and we have struggled with this text (and others) ever since.

So, *Today's Word* is not about this text. The text is clear enough. *Today's Word* is about the paradigm that causes us to read the text as either a problem for our theology or a confirmation of Paul's unity of law and grace. This paradigm is based on an association between the general pagan religious requirement to placate the gods and the Jewish idea of works of righteousness. Pagan religions often view men as victims of the gods. In order to survive in this world, paganism requires that men offer sacrifices to appease the gods and gain their favor. We find this kind of thinking in all kinds of pagan religions, from the worship of Ba'al and Moloch to the Greeks and native Americans. When thinkers read passages in the Bible that described sacrifices and worship rituals, they connected these with pagan appeasement. Therefore, they thought that Israel practiced a more sophisticated version of appeasement theology. This association became the opposing idea to Christian grace. In other words, according to this paradigm, Judaism developed from prior pagan rituals but was still connected to the basic idea of placating YHWH, an ancient god of anger.

Christianity takes a significant step forward by rejecting this ancient pagan idea. According to this paradigm, Christianity rejects any connection between "earning" God's favor and prescribed religious rituals. Therefore, Christianity stands opposed to Judaism.

This paradigm is not based on Scripture. It is based on a general concept of religion, independent of the actual prophetic tradition of Israel. Therefore, it reads the Hebrew Scriptures within the paradigm – and ignores or reinterprets contradictory passages to fit the paradigm. The biggest problem is really right in front of us: How do we take off the blinders?

Unfortunately, many wonderful and devoted believers will not be able to take off the blinders. The paradigm is so much a part of their way of looking at the world, and has been reinforced by the Church for so long, the very idea that there might be another way is so frightening they refuse to consider it. They are sure of their beliefs, so forget the problems and the text. This is the way it has always been. It takes enormous patience, gentleness, yes, and sometimes shock, to remove the fear of examining the text. For some, it just isn't going to happen.

But here's the caution. We can't make it happen either. This is God's arena. We live according to our understanding of His unity, and He uses us to bring about awareness and truth. Insistence will not turn the tide. Love will. It is important to be aware of the paradigm shift that brought about this unwarranted chasm. It is important to know that Scripture is consistent in its grace-Torah perspective. But "love your enemies" is still the authorized way of life. Seek truth. Live Torah. Hope in His faithfulness.

8.

*"Wash yourselves, make yourselves clean; remove the **evil of your deeds** from My sight. Cease to do evil, learn to do good; seek justice, reprove the ruthless, defend the orphan, plead for the widow."* Isaiah 1:16-17

Sacrifices Don't Work

Evil Of Your Deeds – "The mistaken notion that ritual worship could atone for criminality or intentional religious desecration was persistently attacked by the prophets of Israel, who considered it a major threat to the entire covenantal relationship between Israel and God."[43]   In other words, sacrifices don't work for everything.   Religious rituals, even if specifically given by God, don't erase deliberate sins.   Deliberate sins are punished.   That's how they are handled.

Steal something.   Pay it back, with interest.   Lie.   Make amends, publicly.   Harm someone.   Be prepared to be equally injured.   Murder someone.   Give up your life.   The list goes on.   When sacrifices are not efficacious, punishment is.   There are two ways to deal with sins.   Sins done unintentionally are dealt with by sacrifices (when they become known).   Sins done deliberately are dealt with by measure for measure justice.   Any attempt to *excuse* or *erase* deliberate sin through religious ritual is abhorrent to God.   Sin must be paid for!

Take a look at Isaiah's declaration (actually, these are God's words by way of Isaiah).   Do you notice something quite unusual – by our standards?   God calls for *human* transformation as the way of dealing with sin.   Stop doing these things!   Go after the actions that honor the Lord.   There is absolutely no suggestion here of coming to the altar and asking forgiveness.   There is no allowance for living under grace but continuing to act without righteousness.   "Remove the evil of your deeds" does not mean confess your sins in your heart.   It means changing your behavior.

Ha·si·roo roa ma'ale·lei·chem is the Hebrew phrase.   The verb is *sur* (to wash away, to go away, to quit, to keep far away, to stop, to take away, to remove).   It could hardly be any clearer.   What needs to be removed?   Not attitudes.   Not feelings.   Not the "carnal man."   What must be removed are the *actions of evil*.   Clean up the behavior.   Then seek the

---

[43] Baruch Levine, *The JPS Torah Commentary on Leviticus*, p. 3.

Lord. Forgiveness awaits the man or woman who stops doing evil. Don't tell me you're under grace if you haven't been through God's car wash.

9.

*I, I myself, am YHWH; and beside Me there is no **savior**.* Isaiah 43:11

On Purpose Witness

Savior – Go read Isaiah 42:1. What is the purpose of the Servant? To bring justice to the nations – *mishpat*. What is this? *Mishpat* is the word for a judicial decision, a legally binding determination. But it is more than that. It stretches to cover nearly all of what we would call the judicial process. The servant will bring a confronting decision to the nations. He will bring law and order – God's law and God's order. And who are the nations? The Gentiles, of course. The role of the servant, the one who is the faithful witnessing storyteller of YHWH's great acts of compassion, is to take this confronting decision to those outside Israel.

Why does the servant take the message "I am He" to the nations? YHWH gives us the answer. There is no other savior except Him. Without this message, the Gentiles are lost. They serve other gods, gods who have no ability to save. The servant Israel must take this message to the world. YHWH is the Lord. Serve Him and live! Come under His law and order and He will save.

So far, so good. We shake our heads in agreement. Of course the Gentiles (those pagans) are lost. They must come to believe in God and accept Jesus as their savior, right? Ah, well, not so fast. According to Isaiah, YHWH is the only savior. The role of the servant is to bring peace with YHWH, to confront the nations with YHWH's judgment and tell the story of YHWH's compassion. The servant doesn't save. YHWH saves. The servant witnesses to YHWH's saving grace. YHWH brings the nations to a place of safety (*yasa'*). He delivers.

Now this is distressing. New Testament Christians firmly believe that Jesus saves (just read the billboards). If the writings of the Ketuvim Netzarim are faithfully true, then it seems we have a problem. How can God through His mouthpiece Isaiah proclaim that He alone is the savior when the apostles seem to portray Yeshua as the savior? Have you come to the solution? Yeshua must be YHWH.

But this is also difficult. How can Yeshua be the servant who provides the witness and also be the God who saves? Ah, the mystery of it all. Did you think it was going to be straightforward and simple. These are deep matters with deep solutions. Of course, we could pay attention to the text and realize the Israel is called to be the witness. Israel is the servant and all those attached to Israel accept this role. Their purpose is not to simply establish a closed community of purity in worship and work. Their purpose is to exhibit God's grace by living the story of His acts of mercy in their own lives. They are to model what Yeshua modeled, as one man representing the true purpose of Israel for all God's chosen. Perhaps Yeshua plays more than one role in this drama. Perhaps we haven't looked deep enough to see the mystery in the man.

10.

*So one of the priests whom they had carried away into exile from Samaria came and lived at Bethel, and **taught** them how they should fear YHWH.* 2 Kings 17:28

Archery Practice

Taught – Lions were eating people. Not a very pleasant thought. But in Near Eastern thinking, this isn't about lions. It's about offense. The question is not, "How did these lions get there?" or "Why are these lions man-eaters?" The question is "What does this mean?" And what it means, according to the people who lived there is this: we have offended the God of Israel.

What is the solution? Build a fence? No. Hunt down the lions and kill them? No. This is not a scene from *The Ghost and the Darkness*. The solution is to send a priest to these people to instruct them how to shoot straight. The Hebrew verb translated "taught" is *moreh*. It means to shoot or throw. But in this verse, it is about instructing the people in the *straight* way that will hit the target of pleasing YHWH. The priest taught them the proper way to worship, the way that was acceptable to God, the way that shot the arrow right into the bull's eye.

This verb, *moreh*, is derived from the root Y-R-H. It is the same root that produces the word *torah*. To shoot straight is to practice Torah. To hit the mark is to follow Torah. If you want to be spiritually accurate in your life, line up with Torah.

The incident in the history of Israel is remarkable. A priest is sent to foreigners in order to instruct them in Torah so that the danger to their lives will pass. This is a clear case of Hebrew evangelism. But its unusual because a foreign king (Assyria) sends the priest, the priest *lives* with the people and the people are given *Jewish* religious instruction. Not exactly what we would expect today, is it? By the way, the lions stop eating people.

Y-R-H (Yod-Resh-Hey) is the pictograph "What comes from

(or behold) a person's work." Do you want to know the character of a man? Look at how he shoots his arrows. Look at his aim. Look at his target. Forget all the vocabulary and concentrate on the flight of his actions. What comes from a person's work is the Hebrew understanding of character. It's the verbs, not the nouns. Isn't it interesting that Torah is derived from a verb about the target and path of our arrows. Does it help you to grasp the Hebrew idea of instruction in life (Torah) to see the picture of an arrow in flight? Suddenly it not about rules, is it? It's about the artistry of directed flight.

It's about the feel of the tension on the bow, the adjustments for wind and geography, the stretch of the string, the delicacy of the feathers, the razor-sharp point and the connection between eye, hand and target. Torah is the *art of shooting straight.*

Sometimes it takes a priest to show us how. I don't know anyone who learned archery by reading a book. They had to go into the field, string the bow, pull the line and *practice* many, many times before they could hit the target. Torah is an art that requires experiential involvement. So, how's your aim? Do you need some help from an instructor?

11.

*They **feared** YHWH and served their own gods according to the custom of the nations from among who they had been carried away into exile. To this day they do according to the earlier customs: they do not fear YHWH, . . .* 2 Kings 17:33-34

Verbs And Adjectives

Feared – This just doesn't make any sense. Verse 33 says they *feared* YHWH but served their own gods. Then verse

34 says they did *not fear* YWHW. What? How can people who truly fear the Lord practice the kind of fertility cult behaviors described in this section (like burning children alive)? How can the text tell us that these people "feared" YHWH and then turn right around and tell us they didn't fear Him? The problem is the difference between adjectives and verbs.

Verse 33 reads *et-YHWH hayoo yere'eem*. If we carefully analyze the construction, we see that *et-YHWH* marks the direct object, but the verb we expect (*yare'*- to fear) appears as an adjective (*yere'eem* – plural "afraid" or "fearful"). The real verb is *hayoo* ("they became"). So the sense of this verse is not "They demonstrated awe and reverence toward YHWH." It is rather, "They became emotionally fearful of YHWH." In other words, they were scared of what YHWH might do, but that didn't stop them from worshipping the fertility gods. They had an emotional reaction of fear, not a reverential and obedient reaction of awe and respect. They simply accommodated YHWH into their current pagan practices as one more god to be appeased.

We see this clearly in the next verse where the Hebrew reads *eynam yere'eem et-YHWH*. The sense here is "not fearing YHWH." This is behavioral, not emotionally descriptive. Here we have a statement about disobedience, expanded in the subsequent text concerning their disregard for the statutes, ordinances and commandments of Torah.

So we cleared up the confusion, right? The two verses use two difference senses of *yare'*. We are linguistically satisfied. But this isn't the end of the story. Now it's time to reflect on what this text implies. A priest from exiled Israel is sent to instruct these people in the ways of God. They are in trouble. Lions are eating people. They want the danger to pass. But after the priest gives them an archery demonstration and lessons, they simple incorporate what he teaches into their current practices. They might shake a little over this new god, YHWH, but they aren't willing to follow Him exclusively. They just add Him to the pack. As the text says, "To this day they do according to their customs."

What about us? To this day are we still doing according to our customs? Have we merely added God's instructions to our already pagan attachments? Is God just another deity among the ones we worship? Don't we celebrate Eastre (or Tammuz or Astarte) on Easter and Saturn (Mithras) on Christmas? Doesn't Christendom worship human saints and a human mother? Haven't we changed a simple meal into a religious miracle? Haven't we altered the Scriptures time and again to fit our theological needs?

Maybe we need some man-eating lions in our midst? On second thought, that didn't seem to work either. As soon as the danger passed, people went right back to their old ways. Maybe what we need is a radical change of heart – and a new quiver of arrows.

12.

*and there was no man **to till** the ground* Genesis 2:5

False Dichotomy

To Till – A few months ago we explored this Hebrew verb. We discovered that *'avad* is not really about farming. It means "to work," but it also means "to serve" and, in that context, "to worship." So, the same Hebrew verb that covers ordinary effort and tasks is also the word that is used to describe service (to the earth, to God and to others) and worship. This is very important. *There is no distinction between sacred and secular* in the Hebrew idea of what we do in life.

Today I had a conversation with my friend John about this book we have been trying to complete for nearly three years. The book is all about work. It's about understanding how God hard-wired us so that our choices about work will be expression of service and worship. In other words, it's about being who we were born to be, and in the process, glorifying God and blessing others. That is what Hebrew "work" means.

John has a real heart for missions. Perhaps it comes from his family background. At any rate, he is extremely concerned about the burn-out rate among missionaries. Most burn-out is a direct result of attempting to do those things which are not in alignment with God's hard-wired Zone in my life (a Zone is the place where passion and opportunity intersect perfectly). So John wanted to add a chapter to the book, explaining why missionaries and church professionals find it so difficult to enjoy rewarding work. I objected. You might say, "Why did you object when the need is so great?" Oh, I recognize the need, but I objected because there *is no difference* between the sacred and the secular when it comes to *'avad*. To draw an artificial distinction between the missionary on the field and the check- out guy at the Super Target is to endorse a grand mistake. The only difference between the pulpit and the cash register is location. How I express my Zone while glorifying God and blessing others is exactly the same. Yes, my actual behaviors are different, but work isn't about my behaviors. Every task has a different set of behaviors. Work is about living in the presence of God as He created me no matter where I am or what set of operations I happen to be doing at the moment. Suggesting that missionaries are a special case *because they are doing the Lord's work* is just bad theology. Serving people in the check-out line is just as much mission field work as trudging through the bush.

Ultimately, work is not what I do. It is who I am. Nothing grew on the earth because God had not sent rain (an element completely dependent on divine sovereignty) and there was no man to *serve/work/worship* (an element that depends entirely on us). Go to work! Go to church! It doesn't matter. Those are just locations where you practice being God's instrument. You can worship on Monday just as well as you can worship on the Sabbath. The behaviors might be different, but the relationship remains the same.

13.

*Do not **fret** because of evil doers, do not be **envious** of the workers of unrighteousness.* Psalm 37:1

Fahrenheit 451

Fret/ Envious – Paper burns at 451 degrees Fahrenheit. What is your burn temperature? When do the circumstances of life set you on fire? That's the imagery behind *harah* (fret – to burn, kindle, glow) and the implication behind *qana'* (to be jealous, envious, zealous).

Did you notice that the psalmist recognizes the success of the wicked can cause anger and envy among the righteous? There would be no reason to exhort the righteous *not* to become hot and *not* to be envious unless those reactions were quite typical. It takes only a moment's reflection to see just how true this is. There is a constant temptation to become angry over the ones who "get away with it." There is a constant temptation to be envious of those with more than we have. We need to step away from the flame and look at the nature of the God we serve. He is *erech apayim* – slow to anger – literally, with long noses (Numbers 14:18). If God can tolerate the apparent prosperity and success of the wicked, why do we have so much anger over it? Is He not in charge of the rain that falls on the just and the unjust? Is He not the Judge of all Mankind? Why do we fuss and fret over these things? Is it because we are not content with the way God is running the universe? Isn't our anger a reflection of our belief that if we were God we would do something about this? Perhaps we are closer to spiritual infidelity in our presumption than the wicked are in their actions. After all, we are the ones who have sworn allegiance to His Torah. The evil doers may sin in their rebellion but we may sin in our ingratitude. Which is the more damaging blow to fellowship with our Father?

The Bible confronts us with hammer blows to real emotions. We do exhibit anger and envy. What does this say about our confidence in the purposes of our God? Do we trust Him enough to assuage our distress by revealing His character or do we expect Him to do what *we* think is appropriate? Do we worship God because of what He does for us or because of who He is? The man or woman who finds anger and envy in the heart is silently demanding that God live up to his or her standards of justice. How painful must that be for a God who has welcomed such a man or woman into fellowship!

The Psalms help us face ourselves. We read them not simply as poems from the ancient past but as emotional theology. The Psalms are character mirrors revealing the true spirit of all those who care to look. We may encounter unexpected images, images that tell us more about ourselves than about our opponents or the God we claim to serve. But mirrors are needed abrasive therapy. This particular mirror helps us evaluate the issues of trust, contentment, forgiveness, sovereignty and compassion, doesn't it? When you looked, what did you find? Does the Surgeon still need to do some work?

14.

*to the church of God which is at Corinth, to those who have been **sanctified** in Christ Jesus, saints by calling, with all who in every place call upon the name of our Lord Jesus Christ, their Lord and ours:* 1 Corinthians 1:2

Corinthians Again

Sanctified – You've got to be kidding! These people, the Corinthians, have been *sanctified*? No way! They are the worst lot of sinners ever to gather as a worshipping assembly. In fact, they tolerate immorality that Paul doesn't even find among the outright pagans. How in the world can Paul call them sanctified?

The Greek word is *hegiasmenos*, a perfect passive participle of the verb *hagiazo*. The verb itself means "to make holy," but in this case the grammatical structure is really important. First, this verb is in the perfect tense. That means it is an action in the past that has continuing results. Keep that in mind while we notice that this is also a passive construction. That means it is an action *done to* someone by another agent. In other words, the action in the past that continues to have effect today was not our action. It was God's action. He sanctifies, not us. Finally, we see that this verbal form is a participle. It is an on-going action that acts like an adjective. It adds some characteristic to the subject.

And the subject is *us*, you and me and the Corinthians. We have been acted upon by God in the past and that action continues to affect us today. He set us apart, blessed by His name, and the consequence of His action continues.

Something wonderful has happened. God acted upon us. He stirred us toward Him. He set our course. And He isn't giving up any time soon. Of course, we can always resist, rebel and reject, but that does *not* change the fact that God's past act provides for our sanctification. We have to work out the manifestation of being holy in our lives, but we did not have to *establish* it. God did that – and no man has the right or ability to remove God's handiwork.

This is a terribly important lesson for all believers. Inevitably, we will encounter those among the assembly who just don't seem to meet our standards. Perhaps we will encounter these pitiful types when we look in the mirror. But no matter where we meet them, we must always be mindful that God has done a work in their lives and that God's work hasn't stopped affecting them. The game isn't over. The transformation process continues. These are not enemies. They are fellow travelers. Even that person in the mirror is still traveling with us, trying to let God's sanctification become a present reality. What matters most is our compassion for the fighters. We are together in this. We rejoice together. We weep together. We repent together. We exult together. As soon as we stop remembering that God's work is completed, continuing and characteristic, we become the hypocrites we once were. So, take my hand and squeeze it tight. God called us, and I need you.

15.

*These are the **generations** of the heavens and the earth when they were created, in the day that YHWH Elohim made the* *earth and heaven.* Genesis 2:4

Spelling Bee

Generations – Rabbi Robert Gorelik makes an observation about the Hebrew word translated "generations" in his lectures on the genealogy of Yeshua. It is worth remembering. The Hebrew word *toledot* is spelled four different ways in Scripture. In this verse in Genesis, it is spelled Tau-Vav-Lamed-Daleth-Vav-Tau (where the two instances of the consonant Vav act as the vowel "o"). This *full* spelling of the word occurs in only one other verse in Scripture, in Ruth 4:18. All the other occurrences of *toledot* (and there are over 100 of them) are "misspelled." The other occurrences are missing either the first or the second Vav. Is this just a mistake?

Hardly! Hebrew Scripture contains quite a few oddities like enlarged letters, words with missing letters, a word with "broken" letter, extra small letters and stretched letters. Of course, none of these are apparent in translation. In fact, they can hardly be seen in typeset editions. But they are meticulously copied in hand-written Torah scrolls because the rabbis do not believe any of these oddities are accidents. They all have deeper meanings. Let's consider the "misspelling" of *toledot*.

The rabbis taught that the full spelling of T-V-L-D-V-T in Genesis 2:4 indicates that this account of the generations of the world occurred *before* sin entered the world, before death and the angel of death existed in the world. In other worlds, the *full* spelling of *toledot* was appropriate here because the world was not yet corrupted. But a few verses later, when Genesis recounts the generations of Adam, *toledot* is spelled without the initial Vav. It's the same word, but just like the generations of Adam, it has been corrupted.

The spelling matches the status of the generations it recalls. This corruption is true in every other occurrence of *toledot* – except one.

That single exception is Ruth 4:18. In this verse, and only in this verse, the word *toledot* is found in its full spelling. The obvious question is "Why here?" Bob Gorelik points out that in this single instance, the recounting of the generations is the critical link between Boaz and David; a link that is part of the genealogy of the Messiah. Jewish rabbis explain that the full spelling of *toledot* in this verse is based on the fact that Ruth and Boaz are progenitors of the Messiah in the line of David and the Messiah will *restore* God's original creation and remove death from the earth. The Messiah will remove the corruption brought about by sin. When he comes to sweep away sin, *toledot* will be fully spelled out again.

So, you're saying, "Wow. That's so interesting. But does it really matter to *me*?" Maybe the spelling of *toledot* doesn't matter in your routine today, but the subtle intricacy of Scripture does matter a great deal. This is one more incredible demonstration of the amazing planning of God. This is one more bit of evidence that He cares about *all* the details, right down to the spelling. This matters to me today because it tells me that I serve a God who can be completely trusted in the smallest detail.

16.

*"Truly I say to you, all these things will come upon **this generation**."* Matthew 23:36

Born Or Adopted?

This Generation – Yeshua's words are harsh. The

230

generation that rejects Him, refusing to see the truth of His message of restoration and mercy, will suffer. *Genean tauten* are those who were with Him, saw the signs of His anointing, heard His words, witnessed God's endorsement and still refused. There may be many excuses, many justifications and rationalizations, but in the end what matters is only that "this generation" will be judged unworthy.

It is possible to understand Yeshua's pronouncement only within its Jewish context. His statement applies first and foremost to the house of Israel, the ones He came to restore to their purpose and mission. But in a larger context, this declaration has application to any generation that rejects the evidence of His authority and mission. Unfortunately, a quick review of circumstances in the first century and the twenty-first century is more likely to reveal the similarities rather than the differences.

The Jews of the first century:

1. had a legacy of prophetic tradition exhorting them to return to the ways of God revealed in the covenant
2. had God's written word which they avowed as sacred and authoritative document
3. had historical evidence of God's handiwork in the world of men
4. had experiential evidence of Yeshua's impact on men and culture
5. had clear directions concerning God's covenant requirements
6. had signs indicating that something unusual had happened.

Yet they refused to accept His claim on their lives.

What part of this list is not also ours? What reason could be given that excuses them or us? Is our generation also "this generation"? Where are the real differences? Our generation acknowledges there is a God. Our generation has ample evidence for consideration of the claims of Yeshua. Our generation has its own prophets (those who call us to faith) and its scribes and rabbis. Our generation acknowledges the place of the Bible in culture and history. Are we any less excused? Whether born or adopted, do you have any justification for our rejection of the commitment required of us? Does our developed sophisticated theology compel us to obedience or provide us with rationalizations? Where are those who are witnesses (martyrs) today? Are we any less "comfortable" in our belief systems than "this generation"? Has our familiarity with ritual and routine made us any more attentive to the Spirit of the Lord than the routine of temple worship did for the first century Jews? Does the Father still long for your unwavering abandonment to Him?

17.

*But wisdom from above is first **pure**, then peaceable, gentle, reasonable, full of mercy and good fruits, unwavering, without hypocrisy.* James 3:17

What Happened?

Pure – Want peace in your life? Want gentleness, mercy and integrity? Want clear reason and satisfying production? Then start with *hagnos* (Greek for pure). Of course, it's important to know what "pure" means.

Some synonyms help. "Free from defilements, holy, unblemished, perfect" for starters. When we investigate a bit more, we find that the Greek term is almost always the equivalent of the Hebrew *kodesh*, a basic term for purity within the religious sphere. Procksch notes that this is distinct from the idea of ethics since it is grounded in the divine, not the human (TDNT, Vol. 1, p. 89). The distinction is important. When we read "pure" we naturally think of moral acts. We imagine that James is exhorting us to ethical uprightness. But that's not the way the New Testament uses the term *hagnos*. James is talking about ritual purity, about not being defiled before God in worship. In other words, James is telling his readers that the first thing required for wisdom is personal and corporate acceptability before God, the ritual purity described in Leviticus.

Once we realize that James is following Jewish protocol and not speaking about ethical behavior, we see that Torah observance is the basis of wisdom from above. Wisdom, the understanding and appreciation of the practical application of awe and reverence in life, begins with ritual compliance. If I want to enter into fellowship with YHWH, I have to come to Him *His* way. *Hagnos* is the New Testament equivalent of "clean." Everything depends on it.

Now for the "What happened?" question. In the Greek text, *hagnos* is preceded by the Greek word *men* (the phrase is *proton men hagne*). For some unknown reason, the NASB simply leaves out the translation of *men*. The literal translation should be "first truly pure" where *men* emphasizes the perfect quality of ritual purity. Both the Textus Receptus and the NA27th Edition of the Greek New Testament include *men* so there can hardly be a textual excuse for its omission. Now that you know it's there, you don't have to exclude it. The kind of purity James is declaring is the real stuff, the 100% genuine article kind. Why would he need to mention this? Perhaps James' concern with proper behavior, the kind of behavior that does not leave someone "dead without works" requires first and foremost adherence to the proper form of worship. If we can't get that right, what chance do we have for peace and gentleness. Our presence before the Lord is an offense from the beginning. James writes to an audience of Jews and Gentiles who are now in fellowship together under Yeshua HaMashiach. They need to be reminded that the form of worship hasn't changed. It's still vitally important. Life begins with worship and worship begins with being pure before Him. Isn't that still true today?

18.

*"YHWH, Elohey Yisrael, there is none like You, Elohim, in the heavens or in the earth, keeping covenant and mercy with Your **servants** who walk before You with all their hearts."* 2 Chronicles 6:14 (Darby)

Beneficiaries

Servants – God keeps His promises. And God is merciful. That is very good news! But who are the beneficiaries of this good news? Solomon answers, "His servants." How are they distinguished from the rest of Mankind? His servants walk before Him with all their hearts.

'eved is the Hebrew word translated "servant." It usually means "slave," a facet we should not overlook. While slavery did not carry the same nuances that we associate with the word today, the idea of unwavering commitment and ownership stands behind Hebrew concepts of service to another. This noun is derived from the verb *'avad*, "to do, make, carry out or perform." The basic tasks of a slave are to do the will of the master, to carry out the master's instructions and to perform one's duty to the master. Certainly Solomon has these actions in mind when he calls those who experience God's covenant keeping and mercy *avadecha* ("Your servants").

This thought is particularly distressing. Why? Because we want to experience the goodness of the Lord in the land of the living, and this thought suggests that *only* those who walk before Him with all their hearts are the beneficiaries of His covenant and His mercy. If that's the case, most of us (if not all) are not going to make it. Try counting the number of days that you walked before the Lord as His *'eved* with *all* your heart. Actually, try counting the number of hours or even minutes. Days is probably far too much. Can Solomon really mean that unless we are walking before Him with *all* of our hearts, we are not going to experience His covenant and *ḥesed*? I don't see how that can be the case.

Paul assures us, in case we didn't know it already, that we have all sinned and deserve punishment. Paul also assures us that we are no longer condemned because of the grace of God and the obedience of His Son. Mercy triumphs! We are beneficiaries of His love in spite of our faltering commitment. But that doesn't *excuse* faltering. Just as the biblical concept of the wicked describes those who *over a course of time* reject the instructions of YHWH, so the concept of servants describes those who *over the course of time* continually strive for obedience. <u>God's beneficiaries are not the perfected ones. They are the broken but repentant ones.</u> To walk before Him with all of our hearts is to set the course of our lives so that His purposes become our purposes. That takes a long time, but God is patient. He might not be patient with excuses and rationalizations, but He is patient with those He loves to transform. Someday, upon the arrival of the renewed covenant, we will serve Him without wavering. Today we serve Him in spite of wavering.

19.

*"Now, Israel, what does the LORD your God require from you, but to **fear** the LORD your God, to **walk** in all His ways and to*

*love Him, and to **serve** the LORD your God with all your heart and with all your soul and to keep the LORD's commandments and His statutes which I am commanding you today for your good?"* Deuteronomy 10:12-13

Triathlon

Fear/Walk/Serve – Gear up! Prepare! Get going! Three Hebrew words tell you basically all you need to know about attitude and action when it comes to answering life's most important question. What does God ask? Fear-Walk-Serve. Let's look at these three and how they fit together.

Yare is a verb that covers a lot of ground. While it can describe frightening emotional reactions, when it is used of YHWH it usually, but not always, implies awe and reverence. Moses tells us that the *first* action of righteousness is *respect.* If I don't respect who God is, I will not do what He asks. This is a case of saying what I believe but doing what I value. I have to *value* God before I will follow His instructions with my heart. Since compliance is not what God desires, *yare* must be the foundation of all further action. This is the place to begin. Do I *value* God? Actually, do I value Him *as God*? That implies I give Him *ultimate* value in my life. How will I know if I give ultimate value to Him? Ah, easy. His requests come first – always.

Once I have my values in place, then I am able to walk in all His ways. Here the verb (*yalak*) is a metaphor. Its common physical usage (to come, go, walk) is used as an analogy for a way of life, not an occasional step. This is a *direction.* Everyone stumbles. Everyone gets distracted. The verb is about the long-haul, the way that I am going, the day-to-day progress. Eugene Peterson's book, *A Long Obedience in the Same Direction*, summaries the idea of *yalak.* Over time we strive to be obedient to all of God's ways. Of course, there is no logical or moral reason why we can't be obedient to all of His ways *right now*, but the Bible isn't sugar-coated. The text acknowledges probable mistakes. Walking is measured in terms of miles, not inches. But then every mile begins with the span of an inch.

Finally we come to the verb *'avad* (to serve). If *yalak* covers all the inches on the road of life, why do I need another verb to describe what God desires? Isn't walking according to His ways enough? *'avad* is a common description for ordinary labor. Walk and work. That sums it up, doesn't it? Walk and work with your face turned toward God. But *'avad* is not just about work. It's also about service. It's about God's desire for Man to serve His creation. Service in the light of the ultimate values of life is *an act of worship*. Maybe that's why we need this third verb. We need the right attitudes and values; we need to be traveling in the right direction; *and* we need to experience everyday common tasks as a form of worship. We are tri-athletes. Three things are needed to finish the race. All the rest is elaboration on preparation and technique.

20.

and there was **evening** *and there was* **morning** *day one*
Genesis 1:5 (my translation)

What Time Is It?

Evening/ Morning – Our concept of time was *invented* to serve the purposes of the British Rail System in 1847. Obviously, this "railway time" (as it was called) was needed to coordinate the management of the trains, but it did not interfere with "local" time, the time kept at each town across Britain. It wasn't until 1929 that the world adopted the 24 hours global time measurement. Although we imagine that time "zones" have always been part of life, this is not true.

They are less than 100 years old – and they are entirely artificial, determined only by the agreement of various nations to divide the world into roughly 15 degree longitudes. If we look even further back in human history, we find that the mechanical clock was invented until the 13ᵗʰ century. Prior to that invention, time was usually determined by sun dials. Of course, using a sun dial meant that the time of the day varied according to the season and the location on the globe. In other words, *before 1929* there was no worldwide standard to measure time. More importantly, the adoption of a universal standard of time was motivated by the need to regulate production across geography. "The clock, not the steam-engine, is the key-machine of the modern industrial age" (Lewis Mumford).

Why is this little recognized fact so important for us? It is important because once we see *why* we regulated our lives by this artificial device, we realize that the 24-hour day and the 24 global time zones *are completely independent of the biblical perspective.* No "day" in the Bible is 24 hours long. No year is 365 ¼ days. Everything depends on the season, the geography and the designation of *sacred time.* In fact, the only standard measurement of time in the Bible is the Sabbath and its occurrence every seven days is completely independent of astronomical clock time. Clock time is a necessity for modern capitalism. The "week," a cyclical measure not connected to any astronomical event, finds its roots in the Sabbath, established by God, not by the sun and the moon or the rotation of the earth.

Modern research has uncovered another kind of time – biological or psychological time. This time is determined by cycles within the organism. It is our awareness of *internal time consciousness.* It is *not* governed by the clock. Simple reflection tells you that your personal biological clock does not mimic the mechanical clock. In fact, in order to fit into the modern, post-industrial world, you have to force your body to function according to a standard time when your own body rhythms resist such conformity. Your personal wake, eat, work, sleep cycles are not standard. That's why we need *alarm* clocks.

But what if God established a temporal cycle built into creation? What if Sabbath time is really the foundational cycle of all that exists within the human perspective? Isn't this exactly what the Bible suggests? Doesn't Scripture teach us that every living thing is subject to the Sabbath cycle? The Sabbath cycle does not depend on any other temporal duration except that fact that rested. It is also crucial to realize that the first thing Man did after his creation was rest. Man's first task was to enjoy the Sabbath. It should come as no *religious* surprise that the world has systematically desacralized biblical time. The world has altered God's calendar, God's weekly pattern of work and rest and God's view of the day. And to what purpose? So that Man is removed from God's creation even at this most basic level. Clock time has not given Man freedom. It has enslaved him to more and more tasks within the same temporal span. It has removed the sacred *depth* of time by replacing it with the slavery of inexorable motion. Clock time promotes lives of shallow hurry, not lives of contemplative rest and enjoyment.

"The Sabbath – God's claim against our time – implies that time has an ethical dimension."[44] Shulevitz concludes that *not* observing Sabbath dishonors both God and His creation. If Sabbath time is built into the creation itself, dishonoring Sabbath is not only a sin, it is sheer foolishness. It is the death of delight and the worship of toil.

---

[44] Judith Shulevitz, *The Sabbath World: Glimpses of a Different Order of Time*, p. 24

21.

*But **I am poor** and needy, yet the Lord takes thought for me;
you are my help and my savior; delay not, O God.* Psalm 40:18
(Hebrew World)

The Last Word

I am poor – Back up one verse. "Let all those who seek You
rejoice and be glad in You, let those who love Your salvation
say continually, 'The Lord be magnified.'" Doesn't it seem to
you that this is the proper ending? Don't we want the
climax of this psalm to be a declaration of victory? Then
why does the Psalmist add this decidedly negative sentence?
After the shout of rejoicing, why add, "I am poor and
needy"? Why turn apparent victory into defeat?

The Hebrew phrase is *va-ani ani*. Phonetically it's the same,
but the consonants are different. *Va-ani* is Vav-Aleph-Nun-
Yod while the second *ani* is Ayin-Nun-Yod. The first *ani* is "I
am." The second is the word "poor." This particular kind of
"poor" is "oppressed," not necessarily economically
strapped. This poor person is the one who has been
stripped of freedom, who is abused or constrained, usually
as the result of war. The picture reveals the complaint: "to
experience life as work." Perhaps there are a lot more *ani*
(poor) than we first imagined.

The psalm doesn't end with the victory verse because the
victory verse isn't today's reality. Today's reality is life as
work. Victory will come. The psalmist assures us that the
sovereign Lord of creation is gracious and compassionate.
The sovereign Lord of creation is bringing about
redemption and restoration, a time when life will be about
the intersection of passion and production, when we will
serve (*avad*) out of joy and fulfillment. But now the world is
broken. Now *'atsav* has infected our efforts. What was

intended to be both work and worship is sorrow and toil. That's why we are poor. We are prisoners of life out of alignment.

What can we do about this imprisonment? Well, we could throw up our hands in futility. We could just wait for the return of the King. We could pray to be raptured out of this terrible place. We could sing, "This world is not my home." But that's not the choice of the psalmist. He chooses to recognize his present condition. He knows he is *ani*. That leads him to declare that YHWH cares. YHWH takes thought of him. He is not abandoned to this valley of tears. Even here, in the world of *'atsav*, Elohim is our help and our deliverer. Both nouns imply the arrival of reinforcements in the midst of battle. We are not waiting at the station to be ushered out of this world. We are waiting at the battlefront for the arrival of His provisions. The psalmist calls upon the Lord for speedy delivery, not evacuation.

Look around you. Do you see them? The hundreds, the thousands who are prisoners of a life of work. How will you be part of their rescue if all you want is a way out? Are we not called to restore and renew? Do we know the difference between *'atsav* and *avad*? Does it show?

22.

*O Elohim, we have heard with our ears, our fathers have related to us, **the work You did** in their days, in the days of old.* Psalm 44:1 ISR

Praise and Worship Music

The work You did – I must confess. I can't hold it in any longer. The current praise and worship music drives me crazy. It sounds like soap-opera love songs to Jesus. If I hear one more chorus of "like a rose trampled on the ground," I think I'll just turn up the volume on "Get Back." When I recently preached at Glad Tidings Tabernacle in New York City, I interlaced songs from Janis Joplin into the message about dysfunctional families and Adam and Eve. I just couldn't endure the standard three repetitions of the ending chorus of popular Christian music or the syrupy lyrics of force-fitting biblical translations into contemporary rhythms. I wanted the congregation to know that the music of the world is filled with cries for God – and real truth about the human condition. Maybe that's why I love the blues.

But that doesn't mean I don't like the wonder and elegance of biblical lyrics and poetry. This verse is a splendid example of what happens when we *remove* the translation and hear the verse in its original language. What you will hear is a repetition of the suffix ending *nu*, alliterations of *fe*, rhyming of *hem*, *dem*, and nice little phonetic plays like *ata yadha* – all in the first two verses.

Rather than try to examine all the intricacies of this poetic tour-de-force, let's concentrate on only one small example of David's incredible mastery. The phrase "the work You did" in Hebrew becomes a marvelous word play, *po-al pa-al-ta*. Even visually the phrase is arresting with the repetition of the consonants Pey-Ayin-Lamed, Pey-Ayin-Lamed-Tau. "Work You worked" is a better way to capture what is happening in Hebrew, although it doesn't look very elegant in English. And that's the trouble. Most of the exquisite poetic constructions of the Hebrew psalms vanish in translation. So it's not surprising that singing praise and worship music based on the *translated* passages lacks the poetic impact and seems forced. Wouldn't it be better to simply teach the psalms *as they were written* in Hebrew? Isn't that how we learned language in the first place, by reciting rhymes and signing songs?

Now let's think about the message in this little word play. "Work You worked" tells us about the history of God's interaction with His people. Didn't we hear with our own ears those great stories about YHWH's interventions? (You might ask why it is necessary to say "hear with our ears"? How else does one hear?) Don't we have a legacy to lean on? Haven't we been instructed in God's compassion, rescue and deliverance? (There's another poetic construction going on here beneath the surface. It's called parallelism – but that's for another day). If we come to God without His authorized history, we will be faced with a confusing mess. How will we know what God can do unless we know what God *did*? Those stories aren't simply Sunday school attention-getters. They are *our* vital connection to the one true God. We are expected to know them – and know them *very* well. They give us hope when life turns sour. They remind us of His care when we are crushed. They point to His character when our character wavers. "The work You worked" covers everything from creation to regeneration. Time and again the poetry of the Psalms reaches back to the legacy of the works. How can you read David's marvelous poetry if you don't know what he's talking about? How can the Psalms speak to you if the history of God's interaction with Israel isn't *your* history?

23.

*Therefore we have been buried with Him through baptism into death, in order that as Christ was raised from the dead through the glory of the Father, so we too might **walk** in newness of life.* Romans 6:4 NASB

The Will to Believe

Walk – I got an email. "It is certainly not your responsibility to help me but I still struggle with some crippling doubt. I still have trouble seeing, at times anyway, not always, the difference between what we believe and the power of positive thinking. Yes, the disciples all died horrible deaths for what they believed. But no one can prove to me that they walked the earth, much less that what they 'witnessed' happened."

How would you respond to this cry for help? Would you quickly run to your apologetics texts and haul out arguments and evidence for the resurrection? Would you regurgitate Aquinas' five proofs for the existence of God? Would you tell *your* story? Do you think any of those efforts would do any good?

Buried in this email is a thoroughly modern epistemology. That epistemology (how we know things) asks for something that the Western worldview *cannot* deliver – **proof!** What we want is *absolute certainty* **before we will believe**. We will never get it. This Greek-based worldview wants evidence about the world to have the same characteristics as mathematics. In mathematics I can have proof. But that simply can't happen in the external world because the world is not circumscribed with strictly-held rules like the game of mathematics. At best, the world is filled with fuzzy logic. At worst, it is stuffed with paradox.

There is another crucial reason why the expectation of proof is focused in the wrong direction. <u>Proof makes trust unnecessary.</u> No one has to exercise willpower to believe 2 + 2 = 4. There is *no* possibility of doubt about this. Therefore, there is no need to make a willful decision to trust that 2 + 2 = 4. Anyone who doubts this would be considered insane.

Contemporary conviction about beliefs requires *justification before conviction*. But this isn't the biblical (Semitic) approach. In the Bible, I make a commitment and then I discover (perhaps) its justification. "But wait," you object, "that means I could make a commitment to *anything*. To Islam, for example. What keeps me from following just any view?"

The answer is found in the radical difference between our idea of commitment and the Hebrew idea of commitment. Our idea of commitment is that we embrace a way of *thinking*. That's what we call commitment – to vouch that something is true. So, we *believe* that Jesus is God or that lying is wrong, etc. We can *believe* these statements without any real impact on how we act. But the Hebrew view is very different. To make a commitment is to *live a certain kind of life*. To commit is *to walk* according to God's instructions. It doesn't really matter what I *think* about these instructions. If I commit myself to them, then I *do* them, regardless of my current thinking. I am not asked, or expected, to justify them. I am asked to *obey* them – to make them *my* way of living. I am asked to put my trust in these instructions about life even if I don't have *proof*.*

That doesn't mean the biblical instructions are unreasonable. Upon examination, they are very reasonable. I need to follow the Ten Commandments. I need to love my neighbor. I need to honor my parents. I need to worship. I need to be careful about what I eat. These codes of conduct make life workable. But I don't have *absolute certainty* about any of these things. I *decide* to make them my code of conduct. I put my trust in them. This is what it means to have faith – to rely on the trustworthiness of the instructions. And the only way I can do that is to *live by them*. Any other claim of faith – without the code of conduct – is a Western view of justified statements. It isn't the biblical view of faith.

245

Over time we discover that this is the way life on this planet really works anyway. All the really important decisions in life are *trust* decisions, not *proof* decisions. That means there is *always the presence of doubt* at some level, but it doesn't matter. Doubt is the other side of trust. What matters is how I *walk*, and by walking I discover that my trust is sufficient, just like His grace.

"A Jew is asked to take a leap of action rather than a leap of thought. He is asked to surpass his needs, to do more than he understands in order to understand more than he does. In carrying out the word of the Torah he is ushered into the presence of spiritual meaning. Through the ecstasy of deeds he learns to be certain of the hereness of God. Right living is a way to right thinking."[45]

Doubt all you want. Doubt is crucial for the development of spiritual growth. But don't stop doing! Failure to obey isn't a lack of sufficient evidence. It is a lack of oxygen. Without obedience we die.

*This is the reason why *negotiating* with true followers of Islam is hopelessly misguided. True followers are committed to a *way of life*, not a set of rational propositions.

24.

*for there was **joy** in Israel* 1 Chronicles 12:40 (Hebrew World)

The Missing Ingredient

Joy – "Joy is not a theological category in the teachings of most religions and it is never discussed in handbooks of

---

[45] Abraham Heschel, *I Asked for Wonder: A Spiritual Anthology*, p. 120.

theology. Those who are overwhelmed by spiritual solemnity and are unable to forget that faith lives in a constant state of tension between ignominious death and eternal life find it difficult to comprehend the Jewish conception. Even within Judaism the teaching that joy lies in the very heart of worship, that it is a prerequisite for piety, is a scandal to the dullards and a stumbling block to the bigots."[46]

What more can be said? Should we recall that Yeshua does not greet the women who come to the garden tomb with "Shalom" but rather with "*Chairete*." [April 11, 2004] Should we reflect on James famous statement, "Count it all joy when . . ."? Do we need to remember the numbers of times Paul speaks of joy? Yes, it's true, this passage is about the joy of Israel when David is finally crowned king of the entire country, but joy is the watchword of true Hebraic faith. It is the essence of our relationship with the Father and the substance of our message to the world. Without joy, religion is just another way of plodding through the day. If joy is absent from life, life is absent from being.

Simhah is not a feeling. It is the reality, experience and manifestation of overwhelming gladness. It's not simply an inward emotional state. Joy delivers actions. Singing, dancing, shouting, offering praises, prayer, feasting and celebration. Joy is the flow of worship and service. In fact, God *expects* us to exhibit joy as we involve ourselves in His redemptive work. That should give us pause. If joy is the essence of my relationship with the Father, why does it seem so absent in the lives of many who call themselves His children? If joy is to characterize our worship *and our work*, then why do so many of us drag ourselves through the day, hating what we have to do to make ends meet? The Hebrew

---

[46] Abraham Heschel, *A Passion for the Truth*, pp. 51-52.

imagery of joy is captured in a wedding celebration. That's the kind of rapturous exuberance we are expected to display before God! That's what we bring to the Sabbath, to prayer, to His festivals. This is the age of joy, the time of rejoicing.

If you're like me, reading these words produces melancholy. Yes, we know it's supposed to be like this. We are supposed to be flooded with joy. But somehow life saps us of that divine vitality. We catch only glimpses of joyful reality. We experience only moments of bliss. And we think, "Well, that's just the way life is in this broken world." No! That's not the way life is. That's the way we have allowed it to become. If the Lord of hosts *expects* His people to live with joy, then *that* is the reality of our experience. Once again we are listening to that inner voice instead of the external word of the Father. If He runs to greet us as we return to Him, and prepares the finest banquet to celebrate our recovery, why do we withhold what is His – our joy? Get up and dance! Eat! Sing! Love life! Be joyful! That's an order. ☺

25.

*For we are God's **fellow-workers**; you are God's field, God's building.* I Corinthians 3:9 NASB

Work or Toil?

Fellow-workers – For devotional impact, one can hardly improve on Oswald Chambers' commentary on this verse (see April 23 of *My Utmost for His Highest*). With typical aplomb, Chambers delivers a razor-sharp message. A man or woman engaged in the *work* of the Kingdom without a full consecration to the Lord of the Kingdom finds that "there is no freedom, no delight in life; nerves, mind and heart are so crushingly burdened that God's blessing cannot rest." This "work" is nothing but toil because it attempts to replace the sovereignty the Almighty with the planning of noble men. Once more we are delivered to Genesis and the negotiated arrangement of Havvah (Genesis 4:1), a planned solution to her experience of pain – planned without repentance, restitution and reconciliation. It seems that wherever we stray, we don't get far from the Garden.

Chambers rightly notes that God "engineers everything" so that our single goal is not to plan the work but rather to work the plan, His plan of discipling others whom He brings across our daily path. The work which He wishes us to do is not what we concoct or imagine, but rather what He puts in front of us. That's what it means to assert that God *engineers* life.

While Chambers doesn't mention it, we probably need to take a closer look at the Greek *sunergos* (fellow-worker). Paul uses this word to express the *joy* and *happiness* that arrives unbidden when we join God in the effort. We might easily recall once more that assignment given Adam in the Garden. *Avodah* – the work he was to do – was accompanied by worship and service. In fact, it was the homogenization of all three vital elements for the development of what it means to be human. Far too much "work" is done without the essential mixture of these three – and work done in thirds inevitably turns to toil, the destructive erosion of humanity on the wheel of gain and necessity.

Sunergos is, of course, the combination of *sun* (with) and *ergon* (work). Work in conjunction with, work as cooperative effort, work in harmony, work as an expression of unified endeavor. God is not a sole proprietor. One might legitimately ask if He is even an entrepreneur. God is a *company* Man. He is corporate through and through. His objective is the blessing of all through the actions of a few. If we operated according to that cosmic principle, we might find that a good deal of what we *necessarily* do is really unproductive toil. If you discover that there is no joy, no peace, no happiness and no ability to delight in blessing others with what you are now doing, then the chances are pretty good that toil is your mantra and *avodah* has been sent to the recycler.

Chambers teaches us unwavering concentration on God – not on what we think He wants us to do, but on Him – and abandonment to wherever that leads. Paul teaches us that the productive results are not up to us, but we will nevertheless inherit the by-products: joy, peace and happiness. It reminds me of that first labor contract, the one made with Adam. Are you ready to return to tilling the Garden, or do you want to keep pounding sand?

26.

*Give **no offense** either to Jews or to Greeks or to the church of God.* 1 Corinthians 10:32 NASB

It's Complicated

No offense – Paul's exhortation is frankly impossible. How can we not offend either Jew or Greek? We read this verse without allowing it to prick our consciences. If I claim that Yeshua is the Messiah, don't I offend the Gentile who worships a false god? If I claim that it isn't necessary for me to follow the Torah, don't I offend Jews? No matter which way I turn, won't I cause someone to be upset? How can Paul be so naïve?

I'm betting that you have read this verse before and never asked yourself how in the world you could make it happen. I'm betting that now that you think about it, you realize that there must be more to this than simple admonitions to "just get along." To find out what we actually can do not to offend such polar opposites, we need to look a little deeper.

First, let's straighten out the translation. The opening of this verse is *aproskopoi ginesthe* (literally, "not become [one] striking against the foot or causing to stumble"). Of course, we know that *ekklesia tou Theou* is Paul's term for the *qehelah*, the assembly of followers of YHWH. So Paul is telling the readers *in Corinth* not to become impediments to *Ioudaiois* (those born Jewish) **and** (*kai*) *Hellessi* (a euphemism for Gentiles, i.e., those who are Greeks by birth - Hellenists). Does this help us straighten out his exhortation? Yes, it does because now we realize *who* his readers are. His readers are neither Jews by birth nor Greeks by birth. Notice that the potential of offense has something to do with the *ethnic* background of these people. If his readers are not Jews or Greeks by *birth*, then who are they? Well, the division of Jew-Greek as a matter of ethnic separation covers *everyone*. Everyone is either a Jew by birth or a Gentile by birth, so Paul must have some other categorization of audience in mind. What category is left? Only one – the *qehelah* where the differentiation between Jew and Gentile doesn't matter, the *ekklesia tou Theou*.

Now let's see what this means to the audience. How must I act in order not to offend the Jew by birth? Simple. Live according to Torah. But since the *ekklesia-qehelah* was already doing this, why bring up the point? Because as Gentiles came into the *qehelah*, they didn't know the ways of Torah. The new freedom they experienced by not being required to convert to Judaism lead them to declare independence from Torah and this, of course, caused Jews who did not believe Yeshua was the Messiah to discount everything these people claimed. Rightly so, by the way, since it would have been impossible (and still is) for any Jew by birth to accept the claims of any believer in the Jewish Messiah who did not embrace Torah. So we can see why Paul exhorts the *Gentiles* in the *qehelah* not to offend. It is a matter of verifying the claims about Yeshua. Live according to Torah and you will have the right to speak to these Jewish brothers. Don't live according to Torah and you forfeit that right.

But what about the Greeks? Why should the first century *qehelah* in pagan Corinth worry about them? We need to realize that the general spiritual ethos of Corinth was "live and let live." You could believe anything as long as you didn't try to make me believe it too. So the Gentiles of Corinth were not *opposed* to Jewish beliefs, they were just opposed to the *exclusivity* of the

Jewish beliefs. And on this point, Paul's suggestion makes perfect sense. Live by the Spirit, walk by the Spirit, let no man find fault with you and your *life* will become the magnet that attracts others to YHWH. The pagans in Corinth were not categorically resistant to the new *ekklesia* of Jews and Gentiles together. They just weren't ready to believe it until they could see it actually work.

In both cases, Torah living avoids offense. Amazing, isn't it? I wonder why we didn't get it the first time around.

27.

*Therefore, whoever **wishes to be** a friend of the world makes himself an enemy of God.* James 4:4 (almost NASB)

Friendly Reminder (1)

Wishes to be – What do you long to be? What desire do you hold in your heart? James' comment is not about *active* expression and *outward* progression. James uses the Greek verb *boulomai*, a verb that denotes only the passive desire or propensity toward something. Its counterpart, *thelo*, is a verb of deliberate action toward a goal. In other words, James does not require us to actually *do anything* about befriending the world's values. He suggests that all we need is to *wish* we could have what the world offers!

James' suggestion is right in line with the Hebrew idea of the *yetzer ha'ra*. It isn't necessary to actually give expression of the evil inclination. It is enough to simply encourage the propensity and the predisposition for passion without piety. I don't have to use the world's methods to obtain a fortune for my own purposes. All I really have to do is passionately desire such a result. That is enough to keep the fires of the *yetzer ha'ra* sufficiently fueled in my life. That is enough to become an enemy of God.

Too often we think that being a friend (*philos*) of the world means living the lifestyle of selfish consumption. Too often we measure accommodation to the world's values by the actual behavior of the person. We look for the signs of materialism, commercialism and immorality. It is true, of course, that the eventual expression of unbridled passion directed by the *yetzer ha'ra* will result in such outward actions, but this is not James' point. Given time and circumstances, a man controlled by the *yetzer ha'ra* will be uncovered, but James is concerned with the *beginning* of the process, long before the actual behaviors are manifest. The beginning of making an enemy of God is the removal of willful restraint of the *thought* of having what the world offers.

Scripture is the only legal system that provides consequences for inappropriate *thinking*. No other ancient or contemporary ethical structure prescribes such behavior. Outside of the Bible, Man is free to think as he wishes. But inside the fence of Scripture, Man is not so free. Some things are not to be thought of. Some things must be brought into captivity even in their conception. Sometimes it's necessary to have thought police. Dealing with the power of the *yetzer ha'ra* is one of those times. While no court in the world will convict a man of simply desiring to have the wealth, health or influence God has given to another, God's justice will condemn such a man. The desire to remove the restraints incumbent upon the *yetzer ha'ra* is sufficient to deny God's sovereignty and to rebel against contentment. Perhaps that's why the Psalmist asks God to replace his desires with God's desires ("Delight yourself in YHWH and let Him give you the desires of your heart" Psalm 37:4).

So here's the question: What are you wishing for? If you had the means, what would you bring to fruition?

28.

*Therefore, whoever wishes to be a **friend of the world** makes himself an enemy of God.* James 4:4 (almost NASB)

Friendly Reminder (2)

Friend of the world – Who is a *philos tou kosmou* (friend of the world)? This is a vitally important question, perhaps equal to the scribe's inquiry, "Who is my neighbor?" If we have the wrong answer to this question, we might fall prey to the same seduction Havvah experienced.

Here's the simple answer: a friend of the world is an enemy

of God. Obvious, but perhaps not too helpful, until we realize that God has given us quite an exhaustive list of the thoughts and behaviors of those who wish to befriend the world. That list is found in the 613 Torah commandments. A friend of the world disregards God's instructions for living, replacing His instructions with guidance from the *kosmos*. Since there can only be one true God, replacing His instructions with different directions about life can only mean that the replacements come from a false god. To be a friend of the world is to be idolatrous. To be a friend of the world is to serve a god other than YHWH. It doesn't require debauchery, treachery or megalomania. It only requires asserting that God's instructions don't matter.

Was that a body blow? Did that remark suddenly cause you to shudder? If it is true that Torah disobedience puts you in the position of an idolater, are you still able to claim friendship with the Most High God? Do you have a greater appreciation for the dilemma facing Havvah? She wanted to do all that she was expected to do. She wanted to be the best *'ezer kenegdo* she could possibly be. Don't you want something similar? Don't you want to be all you can be, all God intended you to be? But are you willing to manifest that desire *within the boundaries God sets*? Havvah doesn't sin because she is selfish or power-hungry or rebellious. She sins because she desires to *improve* God's plan. The desire is genuine and noble. The means are sinful. She befriends what the world has to offer in order to do what God wants. I wonder how many of us do the same.

Of course, this truth entails two imperatives. The first is that I must know the 613. Not all apply to me, of course, but to ignore or disregard them is an act of rebellion, according to the implication in James. So I must look and see which apply to me.

The second is that I am called to love my enemies. Now I realize that this commandment (one of the 613) extends to those who willfully or ignorantly disregard the 613. They are my enemies because they are God's enemies because they serve another master. And I must love them with such a compelling love that they return to the 613, the fellowship of His community and the experience of His presence. Love of enemies doesn't mean simply turning the other cheek to those who carry a gun. It can also mean caring for those who carry an altered Book.

Index of Scripture References

Skip Moen, D. Phil. (Oxford), is the author of many
books and articles, including:

Words to Lead By (with Ken Blanchard)
Spiritual Restoration, Vol. 1
Jesus Said to Her
The Lucky Life
Guardian Angel
Living in Your Zone (with John Samuel)
God, Time and the Limits of Omniscience

And several thousand pages of Hebrew and Greek
word studies found on his web site

skipmoen.com

He lives near Orlando with his wife, Rosanne.

Made in the USA
Charleston, SC
21 February 2013